Mechanical science for technicians volume 1

Second edition

Ian McDonagh
Senior lecturer in engineering,
Wirral Metropolitan College

Edward Arnold

A division of Hodder & Stoughton
LONDON M

© 1984 Ian McDonagh

First published in Great Britain 1979
Reprinted 1982
Second edition 1984
Reprinted 1987, 1989, 1991

British Library Cataloguing in Publication Data

McDonagh, Ian
   Mechanical science for technicians.——2nd ed.
   Vol. 1
   1. Mechanics, Applied
   I. Title
   620.1   TA350

   ISBN 0–7131–3511–5

Typeset in 10/11pt IBM Press Roman by
RDL Artset Limited, Sutton, Surrey
Printed and bound in Great Britain for Edward Arnold,
a division of Hodder and Stoughton Limited,
Mill Road, Dunton Green, Sevenoaks, Kent TN13 2YA
by Biddles Limited, Guildford and King's Lynn

Contents

Preface

In the second edition of this book, the text has been revised to meet the requirements of the new Business & Technician Education Council standard unit Mechanical science III (U82/040), the aim of which is to extend the student's understanding of mechanical engineering and to develop an analytical approach to the solution of problems involving deformation of materials, dynamics, and fluid flow. Material has been added on shear force and bending moment, and there are also new or revised sections on centroids, first and second moments of area, assumptions made in the theories of bending and torsion, static balancing, and flow through sharp-edged orifices.

SI units have been used throughout in the text, with the following preferred multiples and submultiples:

Prefix	Symbol	Multiplication factor
giga	G	$10^9 = 1\,000\,000\,000$
mega	M	$10^6 = 1\,000\,000$
kilo	k	$10^3 = 1000$
milli	m	$10^{-3} = 0.001$
micro	μ	$10^{-6} = 0.000\,001$

Ian McDonagh

1 Stress, strain, and elasticity

1.1 Types of force

There are three types of force which may be applied to a material:

i) tensile (or stretching) force, fig. 1.1(a);
ii) compressive (or squeezing) force, fig. 1.1(b);
iii) shear (or sliding) force, fig. 1.1(c).

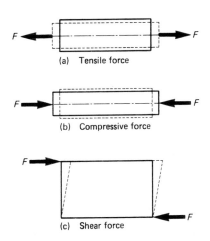

(a) Tensile force

(b) Compressive force

(c) Shear force

Fig. 1.1 Types of force

Tensile and compressive forces are *direct* forces. Direct forces are also known as *uniaxial* forces, since the opposing forces are in line, and these induce *direct* stresses in the material (see section 1.2). Shear forces are *indirect*, since the lines of action of the opposing forces must be separated as shown in fig. 1.1(c) for shear to occur. Shear forces induce *shear* stresses in the material (see section 1.8).

1.2 Direct stress

Direct stress is defined as the applied force F per unit cross-sectional area A resisting the force,

i.e. $$\text{direct stress} = \frac{\text{applied force}}{\text{cross-sectional area resisting the force}}$$

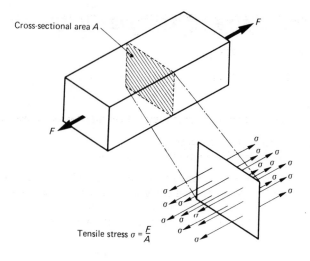

Tensile stress $\sigma = \dfrac{F}{A}$

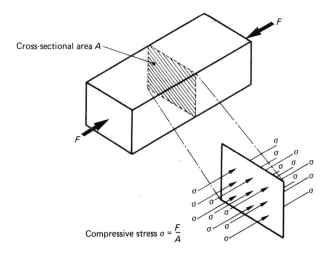

Compressive stress $\sigma = \dfrac{F}{A}$

Fig. 1.2   Tensile and compressive stress

Direct stresses may be tensile or compressive, as illustrated in fig. 1.2.
The symbol used for direct stress is σ (*sigma*); thus

direct stress $\sigma = \dfrac{F}{A}$

which should be remembered.

The basic unit for stress is the newton per square metre (N/m^2). Since this
is very small, the unit meganewton per square metre (MN/m^2) is often used,

2

and the units newton per square millimetre (N/mm^2) and *pascal* (Pa) may also be used. It is useful to remember that

$$1 \text{ N/mm}^2 = 1 \text{ MN/m}^2$$

and $\qquad 1 \text{ Pa} = 1 \text{ N/m}^2$

1.3 Strain
Strain is defined as change in dimension (x) per unit original dimension (l),

i.e. $\quad$ strain $= \dfrac{\text{change in dimension}}{\text{original dimension}}$

Strain may be tensile, compressive, or shear. Tensile strain occurs when there is an *increase* in the original dimension, and compressive strain when there is a *decrease*. Shear strain is discussed in section 1.9.

The symbol used for tensile or compressive strain is ϵ (*epsilon*),

$$\therefore \quad \epsilon = \frac{x}{l}$$

which should be remembered.

Since strain is a ratio of *like* quantities, *it has no units.*

1.4 Modulus of elasticity
All solid materials will change shape slightly when stressed. If a material reverts back to its original shape and size when the stress is removed, it is an *elastic* material. Most solid materials are elastic up to a certain stress limit known as the *elastic limit* — a common exception to this is lead at room temperature. The stress-strain graph for an elastic material in fig. 1.3 shows

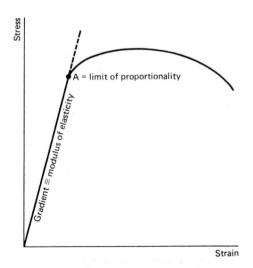

Fig. 1.3 Stress-strain graph for a material

3

that, up to a point which may be at or just below the elastic limit, the graph is a straight line; i.e., up to the point A (the *limit of proportionality*) in fig. 1.3, the stress is directly proportional to the strain, or

$$\sigma \propto \epsilon$$

$$\therefore \quad \frac{\sigma}{\epsilon} = \text{constant}$$

This constant is known as the *modulus of elasticity* or *Young's modulus, E*, for the material,

i.e.   modulus of elasticity $= \dfrac{\text{stress}}{\text{strain}}$

or $$E = \frac{\sigma}{\epsilon}$$

which should be remembered.

The basic unit for E is the same as for stress, i.e. the newton per square metre (N/m^2), though the multiple giganewton per square metre (GN/m^2) is often used.

Table 1.1 shows typical values of the modulus of elasticity for various materials.

Table 1.1   Typical values of the modulus of elasticity. (Note that the modulus of elasticity of carbon steel is little altered for variations in the carbon content.)

Material	Modulus of elasticity (N/m^2)
Carbon steel	210×10^9
Copper	120×10^9
Cast iron	100×10^9
Brass	90×10^9
Aluminium alloy	90×10^9

Example   In a tensile test on a steel sample, an extensometer recorded an increase in length of 0.117 mm for an applied load of 60 kN. If the diameter and the original gauge length of the sample were 15.96 mm and 80 mm respectively, determine the modulus of elasticity for the steel.

$$E = \sigma/\epsilon$$

but $\sigma = F/A$ and $\epsilon = x/l$

$$\therefore \quad E = \frac{Fl}{Ax}$$

which it is useful to remember.

Here, $F = 60 \,\text{kN} = 60 \times 10^3 \,\text{N}$ $l = 80 \,\text{mm}$ $x = 0.117 \,\text{mm}$

and $A = (\pi/4) \times (15.96 \times 10^{-3}\,\text{m})^2 = 200 \times 10^{-6}\,\text{m}^2$

4

$$\therefore \quad E = \frac{60 \times 10^3 \,\text{N} \times 80\,\text{mm}}{200 \times 10^{-6}\,\text{m}^2 \times 0.117\,\text{mm}}$$

$$= 205.1 \times 10^9 \,\text{N/m}^2$$

i.e. the modulus of elasticity of the steel is 205.1 GN/m².

1.5 Stress and strain in composite bars

Consider a composite bar consisting of a steel tube which is completely filled with rubber, as shown in fig. 1.4(a). If the composite bar is subjected to a compressive force F applied through the flat plates on the ends of the tube, as shown in fig. 1.4(b), then the *whole* assembly will suffer a *decrease* in length x, the decrease being limited by the stiffness of the stronger material, i.e. the steel tube. Also, the compressive force F is *shared* between the tube and the rubber, with the tube, being the more rigid, carrying most of the force. Thus, to solve problems relating to composite bars of this type, it should be remembered that

a)   decrease in length of tube = decrease in length of rubber

or   compressive strain in tube = compressive strain in rubber

b)   total force = force on tube + force on rubber

Let subscript a refer to the tube and subscript b to the rubber, then

$$\epsilon_a = \epsilon_b \quad \text{and} \quad F = F_a + F_b$$

But   strain $\epsilon = \sigma/E$ and   force $F = \sigma A$

$$\therefore \quad \frac{\sigma_a}{E_a} = \frac{\sigma_b}{E_b} \tag{i}$$

and $F = \sigma_a A_a + \sigma_b A_b$ $\qquad$ (ii)

which are useful to remember.

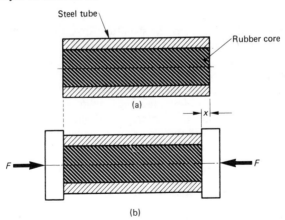

Fig. 1.4   Composite bar

5

Example 1   If the internal and external diameters of the steel tube shown in fig. 1.4 are 24 mm and 30 mm respectively, determine the compressive stresses in the rubber and in the steel when the applied force is 3 kN. For steel, $E = 200\,GN/m^2$; for rubber, $E = 2.5\,GN/m^2$.

Let subscript a refer to the steel tube and subscript b to the rubber.

$$\frac{\sigma_a}{E_a} = \frac{\sigma_b}{E_b}$$

$$\therefore \quad \sigma_a = \sigma_b \,(E_a/E_b)$$

where $E_a = 200\,GN/m^2$ and $E_b = 2.5\,GN/m^2$

$$\therefore \quad \sigma_a = \sigma_b \times \frac{200\,GN/m^2}{2.5\,GN/m^2} = 80\,\sigma_b$$

Also, $F = \sigma_a A_a + \sigma_b A_b = 80\,\sigma_b A_a + \sigma_b A_b$

where $F = 3kN = 3 \times 10^3 N$

$$A_a = (\pi/4) \times (30^2 - 24^2)mm^2 = 254.5\,mm^2$$

and $A_b = (\pi/4) \times (24\,mm)^2 = 452.4\,mm^2$

$$\therefore \quad 3 \times 10^3 N = 80\,\sigma_b \times 254.5\,mm^2 + \sigma_b \times 452.4\,mm^2$$

$$= 2.081 \times 10^4\,\sigma_b\,mm^2$$

$$\therefore \quad \sigma_b = \frac{3 \times 10^3 N}{2.081 \times 10^4\,mm^2}$$

$$= 0.144\,N/mm^2 \quad or \quad 0.144\,MN/m^2$$

$$\sigma_a = 80\,\sigma_b$$

$$\therefore \quad \sigma_a = 80 \times 0.144\,MN/m^2$$

$$= 11.52\,MN/m^2$$

i.e. the stresses in the rubber and the steel tube are $0.144\,MN/m^2$ and $11.52\,MN/m^2$ respectively.

Example 2   A cast-iron tube, 3 m long, is completely filled with concrete and used as a vertical strut. If the external diameter of the tube is 450 mm and the wall is 35 mm thick, determine the maximum compressive load the composite strut can support if the stress in the concrete is not to exceed $2\,N/mm^2$. By how much will the strut shorten under this load? For cast iron, $E = 100\,GN/m^2$; for concrete, $E = 10\,GN/m^2$.

Let subscript a refer to the cast iron and subscript b to the concrete; then,

strain in cast iron = strain in concrete

or $\sigma_a/E_a = \sigma_b/E_b$

$\therefore$ $\sigma_a = \sigma_b \,(E_a/E_b)$

6

where $\sigma_b = 2\,\text{N/mm}^2$ $E_a = 100\,\text{GN/m}^2$ and $E_b = 10\,\text{GN/m}^2$

$$\therefore \quad \sigma_a = 2\,\text{N/mm}^2 \times \frac{100\,\text{GN/m}^2}{10\,\text{GN/m}^2}$$

$$= 20\,\text{N/mm}^2$$

Also,   total force = force on cast iron + force on concrete

or $F = \sigma_a A_a + \sigma_b A_b$

where $A_a = (\pi/4) \times (450^2 - 380^2)\,\text{mm}^2 = 45.6 \times 10^3\,\text{mm}^2$

and $A_b = (\pi/4) \times (380\,\text{mm})^2 = 113.4 \times 10^3\,\text{mm}^2$

$\therefore \quad F = (20\,\text{N/mm}^2 \times 45.6 \times 10^3\,\text{mm}^2) + (2\,\text{N/mm}^2 \times 113.4 \times 10^3\,\text{mm}^2)$

$$= 1.14 \times 10^6\,\text{N} \quad \text{or} \quad 1.14\,\text{MN}$$

i.e. the maximum force the composite strut can support is 1.14 MN.

Strain $\epsilon = x/l = \sigma/E$

$\therefore \qquad x = l\,(\sigma/E)$

where $l = 3\,\text{m}$ and, for concrete, $\sigma = 2\,\text{N/mm}^2 = 2 \times 10^6\,\text{N/m}^2$

and $E = 10 \times 10^9\,\text{N/m}^2$

$$\therefore \quad x = 3\,\text{m} \times \frac{2 \times 10^6\,\text{N/m}^2}{10 \times 10^9\,\text{N/m}^2}$$

$$= 6 \times 10^{-4}\,\text{m} \quad \text{or} \quad 0.6\,\text{mm}$$

i.e. the composite strut will shorten by 0.6 mm.

Example 3   A concrete column of square cross-section, 250 mm x 250 mm, is required to support an axial load of 875 kN. Determine the minimum number of steel rods, each of diameter 6 mm, which would be required to reduce the stress in the concrete to $8\,\text{N/mm}^2$. For steel, $E = 200\,\text{GN/m}^2$; for concrete, $E = 12\,\text{GN/m}^2$.

Let subscript a refer to the steel, subscript b refer to the concrete, and n be the number of steel rods required.

Strain in steel = strain in concrete

or $\sigma_a/E_a = \sigma_b/E_b$

$\therefore \qquad\qquad \sigma_a = \sigma_b\,(E_a/E_b)$

where $\sigma_b = 8\,\text{N/mm}^2$ $E_a = 200\,\text{GN/m}^2$ and $E_b = 12\,\text{GN/m}^2$

$$\therefore \quad \sigma_a = 8\,\text{N/mm}^2 \times \frac{200\,\text{GN/m}^2}{12\,\text{GN/m}^2}$$

$$= 133.3\,\text{N/mm}^2$$

7

Total force = force on steel + force on concrete

or $\qquad F = \sigma_a A_a + \sigma_b A_b$

where $\quad F = 875\,\text{kN} = 875 \times 10^3\,\text{N}$

$\qquad A_a = (\pi/4) \times (6\,\text{mm})^2 n = (28.27\,n)\,\text{mm}^2$

and $\qquad A_b = (250\,\text{mm})^2 - A_a = (62.5 \times 10^3 - 28.27\,n)\,\text{mm}^2$

$\therefore \quad 875 \times 10^3\,\text{N} = 133.3\,\text{N/mm}^2 \times (28.27\,n)\,\text{mm}^2$

$\qquad\qquad\qquad + 8\,\text{N/mm}^2 \times (62.5 \times 10^3 - 28.27\,n)\,\text{mm}^2$

$\therefore \qquad 875 \times 10^3 = 3768.4\,n + 500 \times 10^3 - 226.2\,n$

from which, $\quad n = 105.9$

i.e. the minimum number of steel rods required is 106.

1.6 Stresses due to temperature change

A solid material expands when its temperature is increased and contracts when its temperature is decreased. The change in dimension, x, which occurs with change in temperature is given by

$$x = l\,\alpha\,\Delta\theta$$

where $\quad l = $ original dimension,

$\qquad \alpha = $ coefficient of linear expansion,

and $\qquad \Delta\theta = $ *change* in temperature.

If a solid material is subjected to an increase in temperature $\Delta\theta$, and the resulting expansion is completely (or partially) restricted, a *compressive* stress will be induced in the material. Similarly, if there is a decrease in temperature and the resulting contraction is restricted, a *tensile* stress will be induced.

Figure 1.5(a) shows a rod with initial length l. If the temperature of the rod is increased from θ_1 to θ_2, the length of the rod will then be $(l + x)$, fig. 1.5(b), and the rod will remain unstressed. If the expansion is restricted as shown in fig. 1.5(c), then a compressive stress σ together with its associated strain will be induced in the rod, i.e. the *change* in temperature will *change* the stress from zero in fig. 1.5(a) to σ in fig. 1.5(c), provided that the expansion is restricted.

Referring to fig. 1.5(c), where the expansion is completely restricted,

$$\text{compressive strain } \epsilon = \frac{x}{l+x} = \frac{\sigma}{E}$$

$\therefore \qquad\qquad\qquad \sigma = \frac{Ex}{l+x}$

But $\quad x = l\alpha\,(\theta_2 - \theta_1) = l\alpha\Delta\theta$

$\therefore \qquad \sigma = \frac{El\alpha\Delta\theta}{l + l\alpha\Delta\theta} = \frac{E\alpha\Delta\theta}{1 + \alpha\Delta\theta}$

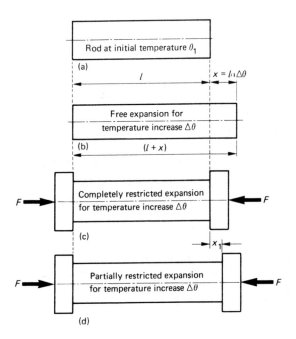

Fig. 1.5 Temperature stress

Since α is very small (typically 0.000 01), the term $\alpha\Delta\theta$ will be negligible compared with 1. Thus the term $(1 + \alpha\Delta\theta) \approx 1$; i.e., if the expansion is completely restricted, then a change in temperature $\Delta\theta$ will produce a change in stress of magnitude

$$\sigma = E\alpha\Delta\theta$$

which should be remembered.

Changes in stress which are induced by changes in temperature are known as temperature stresses.

Notice that $\quad \alpha\Delta\theta = \sigma/E$

i.e. $\quad\quad\quad\quad \alpha\Delta\theta = $ *temperature strain*

which it is useful to remember.

If the expansion is restricted to an amount x_1 as shown in fig. 1.5(d), then

$$\text{total direct strain} = \frac{x - x_1}{l + x}$$

$$= \frac{l\alpha\Delta\theta - x_1}{l + l\alpha\Delta\theta}$$

$$= \frac{l\left[\alpha\Delta\theta - (x_1/l)\right]}{l(1 + \alpha\Delta\theta)}$$

9

As before, $(1 + \alpha\Delta\theta) \approx 1$

∴   total direct strain $= \alpha\Delta\theta - \dfrac{x_1}{l}$

$\qquad\qquad\qquad$ = temperature strain − strain due to stress

But   strain $= \sigma/E$

so, if the expansion is partially restricted, a change in temperature $\Delta\theta$ will produce a change in stress of magnitude

$$\sigma = E\left(\alpha\Delta\theta - \frac{x_1}{l}\right)$$

which should be remembered.

If a material is subjected to both an increase in temperature and a tensile stress (or a decrease in temperature and a compressive stress), then

$\qquad$ total direct strain = temperature strain + strain due to stress

or   total direct strain = sum of strains due to temperature change and stress

i.e. $\qquad\qquad\qquad \epsilon = \alpha\Delta\theta \pm \dfrac{\sigma}{E}$

which should be remembered.

Example 1   The temperature of a steel bush which is initially unstressed is increased from 20°C to 80°C. If the expansion is completely restricted, determine the compressive stress in the bush material. Take $E = 200\,\text{GN/m}^2$ and $\alpha = 12 \times 10^{-6}/°\text{C}$.

Since the expansion is completely restricted, the increase in temperature will induce a change in stress of magnitude

$\qquad \sigma = E\alpha\Delta\theta$

where $E = 200\,\text{GN/m}^2 = 200 \times 10^9\,\text{N/m}^2 \qquad \alpha = 12 \times 10^{-6}/°\text{C}$

and $\Delta\theta = 80°\text{C} - 20°\text{C} = 60°\text{C}$

∴ $\sigma = 200 \times 10^9\,\text{N/m}^2 \times 12 \times 10^{-6}/°\text{C} \times 60°\text{C}$

$\qquad = 144 \times 10^6\,\text{N/m}^2 \quad$ or $\quad 144\,\text{MN/m}^2$

i.e. the compressive stress in the bush material at 80°C is $144\,\text{MN/m}^2$.

Example 2   A spacer in a machine assembly was measured and found to be 200.00 mm long at a temperature of 20°C. After a period of time, the temperature of the spacer was found to be 60°C and its length 200.04 mm. Determine the compressive stress in the spacer at 60°C, if $E = 200\,\text{GN/m}^2$, $\alpha = 11.5 \times 10^{-6}/°\text{C}$, and the spacer was initially unstressed.

For partially restricted expansion, the increase in temperature will induce a change in stress of magnitude

$$\sigma = E\,(\alpha\Delta\theta - x_1/l)$$

where $E = 200\,\text{GN/m}^2 = 200 \times 10^9\,\text{N/m}^2$ $\alpha = 11.5 \times 10^{-6}/°C$

$\quad\quad x_1 = 0.04\,\text{mm}$ $l = 200\,\text{mm}$ and $\Delta\theta = 60°C - 20°C = 40°C$

$\therefore\quad \sigma = 200 \times 10^9\,\text{N/m}^2\ \left[(11.5 \times 10^{-6}/°C \times 40°C) - \dfrac{0.04\,\text{mm}}{200\,\text{mm}}\right]$

$\quad\quad = 200 \times 10^9\,\text{N/m}^2 \times 2.6 \times 10^{-4}$

$\quad\quad = 52 \times 10^6\,\text{N/m}^2$ or $52\,\text{MN/m}^2$

i.e. the compressive stress in the spacer at 60°C is $52\,\text{MN/m}^2$.

Example 3   The gauge length of an unstressed tensile-test specimen at a temperature of 20°C was 50 mm. If the tensile test is conducted when the temperature of the specimen is 80°C, estimate the gauge length for a tensile stress of $150\,\text{MN/m}^2$. For the material, $E = 200\,\text{GN/m}^2$ and $\alpha = 12 \times 10^{-6}/°C$.

Total strain = temperature strain + strain due to stress

i.e. $\epsilon = \alpha\Delta\theta + \sigma/E$

where $\alpha = 12 \times 10^{-6}/°C$ $\Delta\theta = 80°C - 20°C = 60°C$

$\quad\quad \sigma = 150\,\text{MN/m}^2 = 150 \times 10^6\,\text{N/m}^2$ and $E = 200 \times 10^9\,\text{N/m}^2$

$\therefore\quad \epsilon = 12 \times 10^{-6}/°C \times 60°C + \dfrac{150 \times 10^6\,\text{N/m}^2}{200 \times 10^9\,\text{N/m}^2}$

$\quad\quad = (0.72 \times 10^{-3}) + (0.75 \times 10^{-3})$

$\quad\quad = 1.47 \times 10^{-3}$

Increase in length, $x = \epsilon l$

$\quad\quad\quad\quad\quad\quad = 1.47 \times 10^{-3} \times 50\,\text{mm}$

$\quad\quad\quad\quad\quad\quad = 0.074\,\text{mm}$

$\therefore$ final gauge length $= 50\,\text{mm} + 0.074\,\text{mm}$

$\quad\quad\quad\quad\quad\quad\quad\quad = 50.074\,\text{mm}$

i.e. the final gauge length is 50.074 mm.

1.7 Effect of temperature change on composite bars

Consider a composite bar consisting of a copper core A placed inside a steel tube B, with the end faces of the core and the tube being firmly attached to end plates as shown in fig. 1.6(a). When the assembly is at a temperature θ_1, A and B are of equal length l and are assumed to be unstressed.

If one of the end plates is removed and the temperature of the assembly is increased to θ_2, A and B will expand freely to the positions shown in

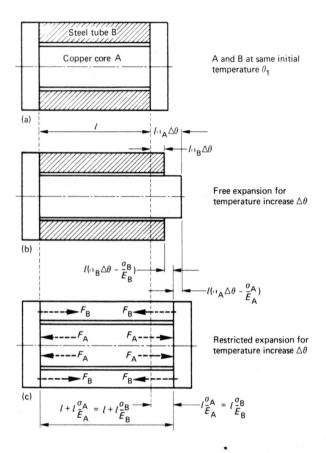

Fig. 1.6 Effect of temperature increase on a compound bar

fig. 1.6(b). Referring to fig. 1.6(b), the copper core A has expanded more than the steel tube B because the coefficient of linear expansion of copper is greater than that for steel.

If, with both end plates in position, the temperature of the assembly is again increased from θ_1 to θ_2, then, provided there is no distortion in the end plates, the copper and the steel will expand an *equal* amount as shown in fig. 1.6(c). Referring to fig. 1.6(c), the length of the copper core A is *reduced* and the length of the steel B is *increased* from the position shown in fig. 1.6(b); i.e. the copper core A is now being subjected to a *compressive* stress σ_A and the steel tube B to a *tensile* stress σ_B.

From section 1.6,

total direct strain = sum of strains due to temperature change and stress

or $$\epsilon = \alpha\Delta\theta \pm \sigma/E$$

12

For the copper core A,

$$\epsilon_A = \alpha_A \Delta\theta - \sigma_A / E_A$$

For the steel tube B,

$$\epsilon_B = \alpha_B \Delta\theta + \sigma_B / E_B$$

where $\quad \Delta\theta = \theta_2 - \theta_1$

At temperature θ_2,

$$\text{length of A} = \text{length of B}$$

i.e.   total direct strain in A, ϵ_A = total direct strain in B, ϵ_B

or $\qquad\qquad \alpha_A \Delta\theta - \sigma_A / E_A = \alpha_B \Delta\theta + \sigma_B / E_B$

$\therefore \qquad\qquad (\alpha_A - \alpha_B) \Delta\theta = \dfrac{\sigma_A}{E_A} + \dfrac{\sigma_B}{E_B}$

i.e. $\dfrac{\text{difference between}}{\text{the temperature strains}} = \dfrac{\text{sum of the strains}}{\text{due to the stresses}}$

which it is useful to remember.

Referring to fig. 1.6(c), the copper core A is exerting a *pushing* force F_A on the end plates, while the steel tube B is exerting a *pulling* force F_B. Since the assembly is in equilibrium,

$$\text{force exerted by A} = \text{force exerted by B}$$

or $\qquad\qquad\qquad F_A = F_B$

If A_A and A_B represent the cross-sectional areas of A and B respectively,

then $\quad F_A = \sigma_A A_A \quad$ and $\quad F_B = \sigma_B A_B$

$\therefore \quad \sigma_A A_A = \sigma_B A_B$

which it is useful to remember.

Example 1   If the diameter of the copper core in the composite bar shown in fig. 1.6(a) is 45 mm, and the internal and external diameters of the steel tube are 50 mm and 80 mm respectively, determine the stresses in the copper and the steel for a temperature increase of $60°C$ if both are assumed to be initially unstressed. For steel, $E = 200 \times 10^9 \text{ N/m}^2$ and $\alpha = 11.5 \times 10^{-6}/°C$. For copper, $E = 120 \times 10^9 \text{ N/m}^2$ and $\alpha = 16.5 \times 10^{-6}/°C$.

Let subscript A refer to the copper and subscript B refer to the steel.

$$\sigma_A A_A = \sigma_B A_B$$

$\therefore \qquad \sigma_A = \sigma_B (A_B / A_A)$

where $\quad A_A = (\pi/4) \times (45 \text{ mm})^2 = 1590 \text{ mm}^2$

and $\quad\ A_B = (\pi/4) \times (80^2 - 50^2) \text{ mm}^2 = 3063 \text{ mm}^2$

13

$\therefore \quad \sigma_A = \dfrac{3063 \text{ mm}^2}{1590 \text{ mm}^2} \times \sigma_B = 1.93\,\sigma_B$

$(\alpha_A - \alpha_B)\,\Delta\theta = \sigma_A/E_A + \sigma_B/E_B$

$\qquad\qquad\qquad = 1.93\,\sigma_B/E_A + \sigma_B/E_B$

i.e. $\qquad\qquad \sigma_B = \dfrac{(\alpha_A - \alpha_B)\,\Delta\theta}{1/E_B + 1.93/E_A}$

where $\quad \alpha_A = 16.5 \times 10^{-6}/°C \qquad \alpha_B = 11.5 \times 10^{-6}/°C \qquad \Delta\theta = 60°C$

$\qquad E_A = 120 \times 10^9 \text{ N/m}^2 \quad$ and $\quad E_B = 200 \times 10^9 \text{ N/m}^2$

$\therefore \quad \sigma_B = \dfrac{(16.5 - 11.5) \times 10^{-6}/°C \times 60°C}{1.93/(120 \times 10^9 \text{ N/m}^2) + 1/(200 \times 10^9 \text{ N/m}^2)}$

$\qquad\quad = \dfrac{3 \times 10^{-4}}{(1.608 \times 10^{-11}) + (0.5 \times 10^{-11})} \text{ N/m}^2$

$\qquad\quad = 14.23 \times 10^6 \text{ N/m}^2 \quad$ or $\quad 14.23 \text{ MN/m}^2$

and $\quad \sigma_A = 1.93\,\sigma_B$

$\qquad\qquad = 1.93 \times 14.23 \text{ MN/m}^2$

$\qquad\qquad = 27.46 \text{ MN/m}^2$

i.e. the stresses in the steel and copper after the temperature increase are 14.23 MN/m² and 27.46 MN/m² respectively.

Example 2   The assembly shown in fig. 1.7 consists of a brass cylinder clamped between flanges by a steel stud. The cylinder is 60 mm diameter × 45 mm bore and the stud is 12 mm diameter. At a temperature of 10°C, the tensile stress in the stud is 60 N/mm². Calculate (a) the compressive stress in the cylinder material at 10°C, (b) the stresses in the cylinder and stud materials when the temperature of the assembly is 40°C, (c) the stresses in the cylinder and stud materials when the assembly at a temperature of 40°C is subjected to an axial compressive force of 5 kN. Ignore the effect of temperature on the flanges. For steel, $E = 200 \text{ kN/mm}^2$ and $\alpha = 11.5 \times 10^{-6}/°C$. For brass, $E = 90 \text{ kN/mm}^2$ and $\alpha = 17 \times 10^{-6}/°C$.

Fig. 1.7

14

Let subscript A refer to the brass and subscript B refer to the steel.

a) Referring to fig. 1.7,

force on cylinder = force on stud

i.e. $\qquad \sigma_A A_A = \sigma_B A_B$

or $\qquad \sigma_A = \sigma_B (A_B/A_A)$

where $\quad A_A = (\pi/4) \times (60^2 - 45^2)\,\text{mm}^2 = 1237\,\text{mm}^2$

and $\quad A_B = (\pi/4) \times (12\,\text{mm})^2 = 113.1\,\text{mm}^2$

$\therefore \quad \sigma_A = \dfrac{113.1\,\text{mm}^2}{1237\,\text{mm}^2} \times \sigma_B$

$\qquad\qquad = 0.091\,\sigma_B$

At $10°C$,

$\qquad \sigma_{B,10} = 60\,\text{N/mm}^2$

$\therefore \qquad \sigma_{A,10} = 0.091 \times 60\,\text{N/mm}^2$

$\qquad\qquad = 5.46\,\text{N/mm}^2$

i.e. at a temperature of $10°C$, the compressive stress in the cylinder is $5.46\,\text{N/mm}^2$.

b) $\quad (\alpha_A - \alpha_B)\,\Delta\theta = \sigma_A/E_A + \sigma_B/E_B$

$\qquad\qquad\qquad\quad = 0.091\,\sigma_B/E_A + \sigma_B/E_B$

i.e. $\quad \sigma_B = \dfrac{(\alpha_A - \alpha_B)\,\Delta\theta}{0.091/E_A + 1/E_B}$

where $\quad \alpha_A = 17 \times 10^{-6}/°C \qquad \alpha_B = 11.5 \times 10^{-6}/°C$

$\qquad\qquad \Delta\theta = 40°C - 10°C = 30°C$

$\qquad\qquad E_A = 90\,\text{kN/mm}^2 = 90 \times 10^3\,\text{N/mm}^2$

and $\qquad E_B = 200\,\text{kN/mm}^2 = 200 \times 10^3\,\text{N/mm}^2$

At $40°C$,

$\qquad \sigma_{B,40} = \dfrac{(17 - 11.5) \times 10^{-6}/°C \times 30°C}{0.091/(90 \times 10^3\,\text{N/mm}^2) + 1/(200 \times 10^3\,\text{N/mm}^2)}$

$\qquad\qquad = \dfrac{1.65 \times 10^{-4}}{(1.011 + 5) \times 10^{-6}}\,\text{N/mm}^2$

$\qquad\qquad = 27.45\,\text{N/mm}^2$

i.e. the tensile stress in the stud is increased by $27.45\,\text{N/mm}^2$,

$\therefore \quad$ total stress in the stud at $40°C = 60\,\text{N/mm}^2 + 27.45\,\text{N/mm}^2$

$\qquad\qquad\qquad\qquad\qquad\qquad = 87.45\,\text{N/mm}^2$

and total stress in the brass at 40°C = 87.45 N/mm² x 0.091

$$= 7.96 \text{ N/mm}^2$$

i.e. the total stresses in the cylinder and stud materials at a temperature of 40°C are 7.96 N/mm² and 87.5 N/mm² respectively.

c) When the external force is applied,

strain in cylinder = strain in stud

or $\qquad \sigma_A/E_A = \sigma_B/E_B$

$\therefore \qquad\qquad \sigma_A = \sigma_B(E_A/E_B)$

where E_A = 90kN/mm² and E_B = 200kN/mm²

$\therefore \quad \sigma_A = \dfrac{90\text{kN/mm}^2}{200\text{kN/mm}^2} \times \sigma_B$

$\qquad\quad = 0.45\,\sigma_B$

Also, total force = force on cylinder + force on stud

or $\qquad\qquad F = \sigma_A\,A_A + \sigma_B\,A_B$

$\qquad\qquad\quad = 0.45\,\sigma_B\,A_A + \sigma_B\,A_B$

$\therefore \qquad\quad \sigma_B = \dfrac{F}{0.45A_A + A_B}$

where F = 5 x 10³ N $\qquad A_A$ = 1237mm² and A_B = 113.1mm²

$\therefore \quad \sigma_B = \dfrac{5 \times 10^3 \text{ N}}{0.45 \times 1237\text{mm}^2 + 113.1\text{mm}^2}$

$\qquad\quad = 7.47\text{N/mm}^2$

and $\sigma_B = 0.45 \times 7.47\text{N/mm}^2$

$\qquad\quad = 3.36\text{N/mm}^2$

The effect of these compressive stresses due to the external force is to

i) *reduce* the tensile stress in the stud,
ii) *increase* the compressive stress in the cylinder.

$\therefore \quad$ resultant stress in the stud = 87.45N/mm² − 3.36N/mm²

$$= 84.09\text{N/mm}^2 \text{ (tensile)}$$

and resultant stress in the cylinder = 7.96N/mm² + 7.47N/mm²

$$= 15.43\text{N/mm}^2 \text{ (compressive)}$$

i.e. the resultant stresses in the cylinder and stud materials are 15.43N/mm² (compressive) and 84.09N/mm² (tensile) respectively.

Referring to the above example, notice that stresses induced by external forces and by changes in temperature can be combined, provided that due care is taken with the magnitude and sense (or nature) of the respective stresses.

1.8 Shear stress
Shear stress is defined as shear force F per unit cross-sectional area A resisting the shear,

i.e.   shear stress $= \dfrac{\text{shear force}}{\text{cross-sectional area resisting shear}}$

The symbol used for shear stress is τ (*tau*),

i.e. $\tau = \dfrac{F}{A}$

which should be remembered.
The basic unit for shear stress is the newton per square metre (N/m^2).

Example 1   The simple riveted lap joint shown in fig. 1.8 contains six rivets, each 8 mm diameter, and is subjected to a shear force of 1.6 kN. Determine the shear stress in each rivet.

Fig. 1.8   Simple riveted lap joint

Referring to fig. 1.8, the joint will shear at the interface CC,

i.e.   area resisting shear, A = total cross-sectional area of all the rivets

$\qquad\qquad\qquad = (\pi/4) \times (8\,\text{mm})^2 \times 6 \text{ rivets}$

$\qquad\qquad\qquad = 301.6\,\text{mm}^2$

Shear stress $\tau = F/A$

where $F = 1.6\,\text{kN} = 1600\,\text{N}$

$$\therefore \quad \tau = \frac{1600\,\text{N}}{301.6\,\text{mm}^2}$$

$$= 5.3\,\text{N/mm}^2$$

i.e. the shear stress in each rivet is $5.3\,\text{N/mm}^2$.

Note that the area resisting shear in a riveted joint is determined by the number of shear planes and the minimum number of rivets which must be removed to break the joint.

Example 2   The double-strap butt joint shown in fig. 1.9 contains eight rivets, each of diameter 10 mm. If the shear stress in the rivet material is not to exceed $20\,\text{N/mm}^2$, find the maximum shear force the joint can support.

Rivets in double shear

Fig. 1.9   Double-strap butt joint

Referring to fig. 1.9, the joint will shear at the interfaces CC and DD, i.e. the rivets are in *double* shear. Also, the joint will break if a minimum of *four* rivets are removed.

i.e.   area resisting shear, $A = (\pi/4) \times (10\,\text{mm})^2 \times 4$ rivets $\times$ 2 shear planes

$$= 628.32\,\text{mm}^2$$

Shear stress $\tau = F/A$

$$\therefore \quad\quad\quad\quad F = \tau A$$

where $\tau = 20\,\text{N/mm}^2$

$$\therefore \quad\quad F = 20\,\text{N/mm}^2 \times 628.32\,\text{mm}^2$$

$$= 12.566 \times 10^3\,\text{N} \quad \text{or} \quad 12.566\,\text{kN}$$

i.e. the maximum shear force is 12.566 kN.

Example 3   Figure 1.10 shows the coupling arrangement for a trailer. If the pin is 30 mm diameter, determine the shear stress in the pin when the pull on the trailer is 8.5 kN.

Fig. 1.10 Coupling pin for a trailer

Referring to fig. 1.10, the pin can shear across CC and DD, i.e. the pin is in double shear,

$\therefore$ area resisting shear, $A = (\pi/4) \times (30\,\text{mm})^2 \times 2$ shear planes

$$= 1413.7\,\text{mm}^2$$

Shear stress $\tau = F/A$

where $F = 8.5\,\text{kN} = 8500\,\text{N}$

$\therefore$ $\tau = \dfrac{8500\,\text{N}}{1413.7\,\text{mm}^2} = 6\,\text{N/mm}^2$

i.e. the shear stress in the pin material is $6\,\text{N/mm}^2$.

Example 4   In a blanking operation, the force on the punch was found to be 20 kN. If the diameter of the punch was 35 mm and the material was 3.6 mm thick, determine the shear stress in the material.

Figure 1.11 shows the blanked portion.

$$\frac{\text{Area resisting}}{\text{blanking force}} = \frac{\text{circumference}}{\text{of blank}} \times \frac{\text{material}}{\text{thickness}}$$

$$= \pi \times 35\,\text{mm} \times 3.6\,\text{mm}$$

$$= 395.8\,\text{mm}^2$$

Shear stress $\tau = F/A$

$\therefore$ $\tau = \dfrac{20 \times 10^3\,\text{N}}{395.8\,\text{mm}^2} = 50.5\,\text{N/mm}^2$

i.e. the shear stress was $50.5\,\text{N/mm}^2$.

19

Shear area = circumference × thickness

Fig. 1.11

1.9 Shear strain

Shear strain is defined as the angular distortion a plane normal to the shear force suffers as a result of the shear force. Figure 1.12 shows a block ABCD subjected to a shear force F. Before loading, the planes AB and CD are normal (i.e. at 90°) to F. After loading, the planes are distorted through angle γ (*gamma*) to AB$'$ and DC$'$ respectively. The angle γ, which is measured in radians, is the *shear strain*.

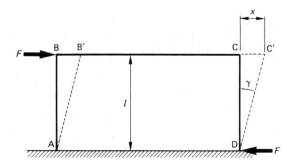

Fig. 1.12 Shear strain

Referring to fig. 1.12,

$$\text{shear strain } \gamma = \frac{x}{l}$$

which it is useful to remember.

20

1.10 Shear modulus

If shear stress is plotted against shear strain, a graph similar to that shown in fig. 1.13 will result. The gradient or slope of the linear portion of the graph OA is known as the *shear modulus* or *modulus of rigidity* for the material,

i.e.   shear modulus $\equiv$ gradient of OA $= \dfrac{\text{shear stress}}{\text{shear strain}}$

Fig. 1.13 Graph of shear stress against shear strain for a material

The symbol used for the shear modulus is G,

i.e. $G = \dfrac{\tau}{\gamma}$

which should be remembered.

The basic unit for shear modulus is the newton per square metre (N/m^2).
Table 1.2 shows typical values of the shear modulus for various materials.

Table 1.2   Typical values of the shear modulus

Material	Shear modulus (GN/m^2)
0.25% carbon steel	82.2
0.75% carbon steel	81.1
0.75% carbon steel, hardened	77.8
Cast iron	60
Copper	48.3
70/30 brass	48.3
Aluminium	26.1

Example 1   The maximum shear stress in a shaft was found to be 45 MN/m^2. If G for the shaft material was 79 GN/m^2, determine the shear strain.

$$G = \tau/\gamma$$

$$\therefore \quad \gamma = \tau/G$$

where $\quad \tau = 45 \, \text{MN/m}^2 = 45 \times 10^6 \, \text{N/m}^2$

and $\quad G = 79 \, \text{GN/m}^2 = 79 \times 10^9 \, \text{N/m}^2$

$$\therefore \quad \gamma = \frac{45 \times 10^6 \, \text{N/m}^2}{79 \times 10^9 \, \text{N/m}^2} = 0.57 \times 10^{-3} \, \text{rad}$$

i.e. the maximum shear strain was 0.57×10^{-3} radians.

Example 2 The apparatus shown in fig. 1.14 was used to determine the shear modulus of rubber. When the mean load was 100 N, the deflection was 1.2 mm. Calculate the shear modulus of the rubber.

Fig. 1.14 Apparatus to determine shear modulus of rubber

Referring to fig. 1.14,

area resisting shear $= 300 \, \text{mm} \times 25 \, \text{mm}$

$= 7500 \, \text{mm}^2$

Shear stress $\tau = F/A$

where $\quad F = 100 \, \text{N}$

$$\therefore \quad \tau = \frac{100 \, \text{N}}{7500 \, \text{mm}^2} = 0.0133 \, \text{N/mm}^2$$

22

After loading, the faces AB and DC are distorted through angle γ to AB'
and DC' respectively.

$$\therefore \quad \gamma = \frac{1.2\,\text{mm}}{100\,\text{mm}} = 0.012\,\text{rad}$$

Shear modulus $G = \tau/\gamma$

$$= \frac{0.0133\,\text{N/mm}^2}{0.012\,\text{rad}}$$

$$= 1.11\,\text{N/mm}^2 \quad \text{or} \quad 1.11\,\text{MN/m}^2$$

i.e. the shear modulus of the rubber is $1.11\,\text{MN/m}^2$.

1.11 Poisson's ratio

As the circular specimen shown in fig. 1.15 is stretched, its diameter will be
reduced, i.e. a compressive strain will be induced in the material at right
angles to the line of action of the tensile force. This strain, known as the
lateral strain, is directly proportional to the direct or *longitudinal* strain
produced by the force; i.e. lateral strain is directly proportional to
longitudinal strain.

Fig. 1.15 Lateral compression due to longitudinal force

Let $\quad \epsilon_x$ = longitudinal strain $\quad$ and $\quad \epsilon_y$ = lateral strain

then $\quad \epsilon_y \propto \epsilon_x$

or $\quad \epsilon_y = \nu \epsilon_x$

The constant ν (*nu*) is known as Poisson's ratio,

i.e. $\quad$ Poisson's ratio $\nu = \dfrac{\epsilon_y}{\epsilon_x} = \dfrac{\text{lateral strain}}{\text{longitudinal strain}}$

which should be remembered.

Since it is a ratio of like quantities, Poisson's ratio has no units. For
metals, Poisson's ratio can vary between 0.25 and 0.33.

Example A tensile-test specimen of diameter 10 mm is subjected to an axial
force of 15 kN. If E for the material is $207\,\text{kN/mm}^2$ and Poisson's ratio is
0.29, determine the lateral strain and the change in diameter.

Longitudinal strain $\epsilon_x = \sigma/E = F/(AE)$

where $\quad F = 15\,\text{kN} = 15 \times 10^3\,\text{N} \qquad A = (\pi/4) \times (10\,\text{mm})^2 = 78.54\,\text{mm}^2$

and $\quad E = 207\,\text{kN/mm}^2 = 207 \times 10^3\,\text{N/mm}^2$

$$\therefore \quad \epsilon_x = \frac{15 \times 10^3\,\text{N}}{78.54\,\text{mm}^2 \times 207 \times 10^3\,\text{N/mm}^2}$$

$$= 9.23 \times 10^{-4}$$

Lateral strain $= \nu \times$ longitudinal strain

or $\qquad \epsilon_y = \nu\,\epsilon_x$

where $\quad \nu = 0.29$

$\therefore \quad \epsilon_y = 0.29 \times 9.23 \times 10^{-4}$

$\qquad = 2.68 \times 10^{-4}$

i.e. the lateral strain is 2.68×10^{-4}.

Change in diameter $=$ original diameter $\times$ lateral strain

$$= 10\,\text{mm} \times 2.68 \times 10^{-4}$$

$$= 2.68 \times 10^{-3}\,\text{mm}$$

i.e. the change in diameter is 2.68×10^{-3} mm.

1.12 Two-dimensional stress

Consider the stressed element shown in fig. 1.16(a). The strains induced in the element by σ_x and σ_y each acting alone are shown in figs 1.16(b) and 1.16(c) respectively. Figure 1.16(d) illustrates the total or resultant strains in the directions of σ_x and σ_y.

Referring to fig. 1.16(d), the resultant strain in the direction of σ_x is given by

$$\epsilon_x = \frac{\sigma_x}{E} - \nu\,\frac{\sigma_y}{E}$$

and the resultant strain in the direction of σ_y is given by

$$\epsilon_y = \frac{\sigma_y}{E} - \nu\,\frac{\sigma_x}{E}$$

which should be remembered.

Example The element shown in fig. 1.17 is subjected to two mutually perpendicular stresses of magnitude $50\,\text{MN/m}^2$ (tensile) and $35\,\text{MN/m}^2$ (compressive) respectively. If $E = 120\,\text{GN/m}^2$ and $\nu = 0.28$, determine the resultant strains in the directions of the stresses.

24

Fig. 1.16 Two-dimensional stress

Fig. 1.17

Let $\sigma_x = 50\,\text{MN/m}^2 = 50 \times 10^6\,\text{N/m}^2$

and $\sigma_y = -(35\,\text{MN/m}^2) = -(35 \times 10^6)\,\text{N/m}^2$

(σ_y is negative since the stress is compressive and of *opposite* sign to the tensile stress.)

then $\epsilon_x = \sigma_x/E - \nu(\sigma_y/E)$

25

where $E = 120\,\text{GN/m}^2 = 120 \times 10^9\,\text{N/m}^2$ and $\nu = 0.28$

$$\therefore\quad \epsilon_x = \left(\frac{50 \times 10^6\,\text{N/m}^2}{120 \times 10^9\,\text{N/m}^2}\right) - \left(0.28 \times \frac{-(35 \times 10^6)\,\text{N/m}^2}{120 \times 10^9\,\text{N/m}^2}\right)$$

$$= (4.17 \times 10^{-4}) + (0.82 \times 10^{-4})$$

$$= 4.99 \times 10^{-4}$$

i.e. the strain in the direction of the $50\,\text{MN/m}^2$ stress is 4.99×10^{-4}.

Also, $\quad \epsilon_y = \sigma_y/E - \nu(\sigma_x/E)$

$$= \left(\frac{-(35 \times 10^6)\,\text{N/m}^2}{120 \times 10^9\,\text{N/m}^2}\right) - \left(0.28 \times \frac{50 \times 10^6\,\text{N/m}^2}{120 \times 10^9\,\text{N/m}^2}\right)$$

$$= (-2.92 \times 10^{-4}) - (1.17 \times 10^{-4})$$

$$= -4.09 \times 10^{-4}$$

(the minus sign indicating that the strain is compressive)
i.e. the total strain in the direction of the $35\,\text{MN/m}^2$ stress is 4.09×10^{-4} and it is compressive.

Exercises on chapter 1

1 A composite bar is 350 mm long and consists of a copper tube butt-welded to the end face of a steel bar. The tube dimensions are 30 mm diameter x 20 mm bore x 200 mm long, and the steel bar is 30 mm diameter and 150 mm long. If the bar supports an axial force of 4 kN, determine (a) the stresses in the copper and the steel, (b) the change in length of the composite bar. For steel, $E = 200\,\text{GN/m}^2$; for copper, $E = 120\,\text{GN/m}^2$.
[$10.2\,\text{N/mm}^2$; $5.66\,\text{N/mm}^2$; $0.0212\,\text{mm}$]
2 A steel oil-filter casing is held in place by a brass stud, 10 mm diameter and of effective length 125 mm. The outside diameter of the casing is 55 mm, the material is 2.5 mm thick, and its effective length is 125 mm. If the clamping force on the stud at a temperature of $15°C$ is 1500 N, at what oil temperature will the filter just begin to leak? Ignore the effect of the filter end plate and take E for brass and steel as $90\,\text{GN/m}^2$ and $200\,\text{GN/m}^2$ respectively. The coefficients of linear expansion for brass and steel are $16 \times 10^{-6}/°C$ and $12 \times 10^{-6}/°C$. [$72.6°C$]
3 A concrete pillar, 250 mm diameter and 3 m long, is reinforced by steel rods, each 10 mm diameter and 3 m long. If the maximum stress in the concrete is not to exceed $5\,\text{N/mm}^2$, calculate the minimum number of steel rods required in order that the reinforced pillar can support an axial load of 600 kN. How much will the pillar shorten under this load? For steel, $E = 200\,\text{kN/mm}^2$; for concrete, $E = 10\,\text{kN/mm}^2$. [48; $1.49\,\text{mm}$]
4 Two steel plates are riveted together using ten 8 mm diameter rivets. If the shear stress in the rivet material is limited to $5\,\text{N/mm}^2$, determine the maximum shearing force which the joint can support. [$2513\,\text{N}$]
5 The clevis pin in a steel sling is 30 mm diameter and is in double shear. What is the maximum load the pin can support if the shear stress is limited to

10 N/mm^2?   [14 137 N]

6   The shear stress in a shaft transmitting power is 2.6 N/mm^2. If G for the shaft material is 79 GN/m^2, determine the shear strain.   [3.3×10^{-5} rad]

7   At a point in a stressed material, the shear strain was found to be 4.8×10^{-4} rad. If the shear modulus for the material is 60 kN/mm^2, what was the shear stress?   [28.8 N/mm^2]

8   In an experiment to determine the shear modulus of steel, the following observations were made:

Shear stress (N/mm^2)	5	10	15	20	25
Shear strain (rad x 10^{-5})	6.3	12.9	19.2	25.7	32.0

Plot a graph of shear stress against shear strain, and hence determine the shear modulus for the steel.   [78 GN/m^2]

9   A composite bar consists of a brass strip, 20 mm wide and 4 mm thick, sandwiched between two steel strips each 20 mm wide and 3 mm thick, the three strips being held together by two rivets each 6 mm diameter and 50 mm apart. The shear stress at failure in the rivet material is 8.49 N/mm^2. If the assembly was made at a temperature of $16°\text{C}$ and is now heated, at what temperature will the rivets fail? What will be the distance between the rivets at the instant of failure? Ignore the effect of temperature on the rivet material. For steel, $E = 200 \text{ kN/mm}^2$ and $\alpha = 11.5 \times 10^{-6}/°\text{C}$. For brass, $E = 90 \text{ kN/mm}^2$ and $\alpha = 16 \times 10^{-6}/°\text{C}$.   [$35.3°\text{C}$; 50.012 mm]

10   A steel rope of diameter 25 mm and length 4 m is subjected to a tensile force of 30 kN. If the modulus of elasticity and Poisson's ratio for the material are 200 GN/m^2 and 0.28 respectively, determine the final length and diameter of the rope.   [4.0012 m; 24.998 mm]

11   The clearance on diameter between a bearing and a shaft of diameter 200 mm is 0.04 mm. If the modulus of elasticity and Poisson's ratio for the shaft material are 207 GN/m^2 and 0.29 respectively, determine the axial force which must be applied to the shaft to reduce the diametral clearance to 0.01 mm.   [3.36 MN]

12   A material is subjected to two mutually perpendicular tensile stresses of magnitudes 40 N/mm^2 and 60 N/mm^2 respectively. If Poisson's ratio is 0.3 and the modulus of elasticity is 150 kN/mm^2, determine the total strains in the directions of the stresses.   [1.47×10^{-4}; 3.2×10^{-4}]

13   At a point in a material, there is a compressive stress of 60 N/mm^2 and perpendicular to this stress a tensile strain of 2×10^{-4}. Determine (a) the magnitude and sense of the stress in the plane of the tensile strain, (b) the magnitude and sense of the strain in the direction of the compressive stress. For the material, $E = 207 \text{ kN/mm}^2$ and $\nu = 0.28$. [24.6 N/mm^2 (tensile); 3.23×10^{-4} (compressive)]

14   A short concrete column has a square cross-section of side 400 mm and is reinforced by four steel bars, each 20 mm diameter. If the ratio E_steel to E_concrete is 15:1, calculate the compressive stress in the concrete when the column supports an axial load of 1.4 MN.   [7.88 MN/m^2]

15   A double-strap butt joint contains a total of twelve rivets, each 5 mm diameter. Calculate the shear stress in each rivet when the joint is subjected to a shearing force of 1 kN.   [4.24 N/mm^2]

16 Define Poisson's ratio.

At a point in a material, there is a tensile strain of 8×10^{-4} and perpendicular to this strain a compressive strain of 3×10^{-4}. If Poisson's ratio is 0.3 and the modulus of elasticity is $150 \, \text{GN/m}^2$, calculate the stresses in the direction of the strains.
$[117 \, \text{MN/m}^2$ (tensile); $9.89 \, \text{MN/m}^2$ (compressive)$]$

17 A steel strip, 50 mm x 10 mm x 200 mm long, is subjected to an axial tensile force of 125 kN. If Poisson's ratio = 0.3 and $E = 200 \, \text{GN/m}^2$, determine the change in volume. [$50 \, \text{mm}^3$ increase]

18 A steel tube having an outside diameter of 75 mm is 'shrink-fitted' on to a copper cylinder of 65 mm outside diameter and 40 mm bore. After assembly, the ends of the composite tube are machined to give an overall length of 150 mm. If the assembly is subjected to a temperature increase of $50°C$, determine the shear stress at the copper–steel interface, assuming that the expansion of the copper and of the steel are the same. For the steel, $E = 200 \, \text{GN/m}^2$ and $\alpha = 11.5 \times 10^{-6}/°C$. For the copper, $E = 120 \, \text{GN/m}^2$ and $\alpha = 16.5 \times 10^{-6}/°C$. $[0.95 \, \text{N/mm}^2]$

19 A brass sleeve having an outside diameter of 40 mm is screwed on to a steel stud such that the mean interface diameter is 24 mm. The ends of the assembly are then machined so that the two materials are the same length. If the temperature of the assembly is increased by $60°C$ and the assembly is then subjected to a compressive force of 40 kN, calculate the magnitude and sense of the stresses in the steel and the brass. Assume there to be no back-lash in the screw thread. For steel, take $E = 200 \, \text{kN/mm}^2$ and $\alpha = 11.5 \times 10^{-6}/°C$; for brass, take $E = 90 \, \text{kN/mm}^2$ and $\alpha = 16 \times 10^{-6}/°C$. [Steel, $25.1 \, \text{N/mm}^2$ (compressive); brass, $35.6 \, \text{N/mm}^2$ (compressive)]

20 A steel rod, 30 mm in diameter, is threaded at each end and is located inside a copper tube, outside diameter 50 mm and wall thickness 6 mm. Thick washers and a nut are located on each end of the rod and the nuts are tightened, thus clamping the tube between the washers. At a temperature of $10°C$, the compressive stress in the copper tube is $25 \, \text{N/mm}^2$. Calculate the magnitude and sense of the stresses in the copper and the steel when the temperature of the assembly is $50°C$. With the assembly at $50°C$, calculate the resultant stresses in the copper and the steel when an axial tensile force of 12 kN is applied to (a) the steel rod, (b) the copper tube. Ignore the effect of temperature change on the nuts and the washers. For steel, take $E = 200 \, \text{kN/mm}^2$ and $\alpha = 11.5 \times 10^{-6}/°C$; for copper, take $E = 120 \, \text{kN/mm}^2$ and $\alpha = 16.5 \times 10^{-6}/°C$. [$39.1 \, \text{N/mm}^2$ (compressive), $45.7 \, \text{N/mm}^2$ (tensile); (a) $24.6 \, \text{N/mm}^2$ (compressive), $62.7 \, \text{N/mm}^2$ (tensile); (b) $33.1 \, \text{N/mm}^2$ (compressive), $55.7 \, \text{N/mm}^2$ (tensile)]

2 Shear force, bending moment, and bending stress

2.1 Introduction
The terms *shear force* and *bending moment* are applied to *beams*, a beam being part of a structure which supports *transverse loads*, i.e. loads which are perpendicular to the length of the beam.

2.2 Equilibrium of beams
For a horizontal beam to be at rest (i.e. in equilibrium) when acted upon by transverse forces, the following conditions *must* be satisfied:

a) the sum of the clockwise moments about *any* point must equal the sum of the anticlockwise moments about the *same* point,

i.e. $\sum \begin{matrix}\text{clockwise moments} \\ \text{about a point}\end{matrix} = \sum \begin{matrix}\text{anticlockwise moments} \\ \text{about the same point}\end{matrix}$

(the symbol Σ (capital *sigma*) means 'sum of');

b) the sum of the forces acting upwards must equal the sum of the forces acting downwards,

i.e. Σ upward forces = Σ downward forces

2.3 Beam reactions
Beams may be supported in a number of ways:

a) simply supported (fig. 2.1(a));
b) built-in at both ends (fig. 2.1(b)) – this type of beam is called an *encastré* beam;
c) built-in at one end only (fig. 2.1(c)) – this type of beam is called a *cantilever*;
d) built-in at one end and simply supported at the other (fig. 2.1(d)) – this type of beam is called a *propped cantilever*.

At the points of support, the downward forces acting on the beam are resisted by forces acting upwards. These upward forces are known as the *beam reactions* or simply *reactions*. The reactions for built-in or encastré beams and for propped cantilevers are statically indeterminate (i.e. they cannot be found by use only of the conditions for equilibrium stated in section 2.2).

Example 1 A beam ABCDE is 11 m long and is simply supported at A and D. The beam carries point loads of magnitude 100 kN and 80 kN at B and E respectively, together with a uniformly distributed load (u.d.l.) of 20 kN/m

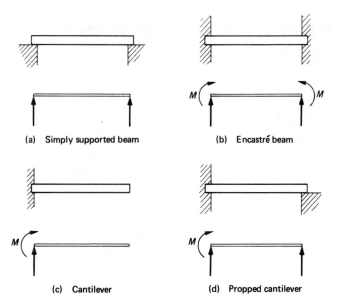

(a) Simply supported beam

(b) Encastré beam

(c) Cantilever

(d) Propped cantilever

Fig. 2.1

between C and D. AB = DE = 1 m, and CD = 6 m. Calculate the reactions at A and D.

From the description, the loading diagram shown in fig. 2.2 may be drawn.

For the purpose of calculating the reactions, the u.d.l. may be replaced by a point load of magnitude 6 m x 20 kN/m = 120 kN acting at the mid-point of the u.d.l. and shown dotted in fig. 2.2.

Taking moments about A,

$$\Sigma \text{ anticlockwise moments} = \Sigma \text{ clockwise moments}$$

$$\therefore \quad 10R_D = 100 \text{kN} \times 1 \text{m} + 120 \text{kN} \times 7 \text{m} + 80 \text{kN} \times 11 \text{m}$$

$$= (100 + 840 + 880) \text{kNm}$$

$$\therefore \quad R_D = 182 \text{kN}$$

Fig. 2.2

30

Σ upward forces = Σ downward forces

$\therefore$ $R_A + 182\text{kN}$ = $(100 + 120 + 80)\text{kN}$

$\therefore$ R_A = 118kN

i.e. the reactions are 118kN at A and 182kN at D.

Example 2   For the loaded cantilever shown in fig. 2.3, calculate the reaction at the point A.

Fig. 2.3

Since there is only one vertical reaction, this is found using

Σ upward forces = Σ downward forces

$\therefore$ R_A = $(10\text{kN/m} \times 4\text{m}) + 60\text{kN}$

                  = 100kN

i.e. the vertical reaction at A is 100kN.

2.4 Shear force and shear-force diagrams

The shear force at any section in a loaded beam which is in equilibrium is defined as the algebraic sum of all the vertical forces acting *either* to the *left* of the section *or* to the *right* of the section being considered (*not both together*),

i.e.   shear force at = $\displaystyle\sum$ external vertical forces acting *either* to the left
        any section   *or* to the right of the section

The symbol used for shear force is Q.

When calculating shear force, the sign convention shown in fig. 2.4 is used. Referring to fig. 2.4,

a) when considering shear force to the *left* of XX, upward forces are positive and downward forces are *negative*;

b) when considering shear force to the *right* of XX, upward forces are *negative* and downward forces are *positive*.

The distribution of shear force along the length of a beam may be illustrated graphically on a *shear-force diagram* (SF diagram).

31

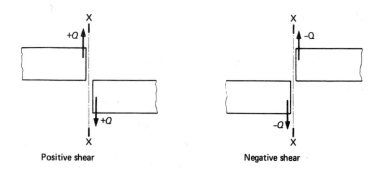

Positive shear   Negative shear

Fig. 2.4   Shear-force sign convention

Example   For the loaded beam shown in fig. 2.5, calculate the shear force in sections AB, BD, and DE and thus determine the shear force at point C. Illustrate the distribution of the shear force on a SF diagram.

Fig. 2.5

For the purpose of calculating the reactions, the u.d.l. may be replaced by the point load of magnitude $6m \times 20kN/m = 120kN$ shown dotted in fig. 2.5.

Taking moments about A,

$$\Sigma \text{ anticlockwise moments } = \Sigma \text{ clockwise moments}$$

$$\therefore \quad\quad\quad 8R_E = 80kN \times 2m + 120kN \times 5m + 80kN \times 6m$$

$$= 1240kNm$$

$$\therefore \quad\quad\quad R_E = 155kN$$

$$\Sigma \text{ upward forces } = \Sigma \text{ downward forces}$$

$$\therefore \quad R_A + 155kN = (80 + 120 + 80)kN$$

$$\therefore \quad\quad\quad R_A = 125kN$$

$$Q_{XX} = \Sigma \text{ external forces to } left \text{ of XX}$$

Consider section AB (fig. 2.6):
At any value for x between 0 and 2 measured from A,

$$Q_{XX} = R_A = 125\,\text{kN}$$

Fig. 2.6

i.e. at A, $x = 0$

$$Q_A = 125\,\text{kN (upwards)}$$

and at B, $x = 2$

$$Q_B = 125\,\text{kN (upwards)}$$

i.e. between A and B the shear force is constant and of magnitude 125 kN.

Consider section BD (fig. 2.7):
For any value of x between 2 and 6 measured from A,

$$Q_{XX} = 125\,\text{kN} - 80\,\text{kN} - 20\,\text{kN/m} \times (x - 2)\text{m}$$
$$= (85 - 20x)\,\text{kN}$$

Fig. 2.7

i.e. at B, $x = 2$

$$\therefore \quad Q_B = (85 - 20 \times 2)\,\text{kN}$$
$$= 45\,\text{kN (upwards)}$$

33

and at D, $x = 6$

$$\therefore \quad Q_D = (85 - 20 \times 6)\text{kN}$$

$$= -35\text{kN (downwards)}$$

i.e. between B and D the shear force will change uniformly with x, producing a straight line having a slope or gradient of 20 kN/m as shown in the shear-force diagram (fig. 2.9).

At the point C, $x = 4$

$$\therefore \quad Q_C = (85 - 20 \times 4)\text{kN}$$

$$= 5\text{kN (upwards)}$$

Consider section DE (fig. 2.8):
For any value of x between 6 and 8 measured from A,

$$Q_{XX} = 125\text{kN} - 80\text{kN} - 20\text{kN/m} \times (x - 2)\text{m} - 80\text{kN}$$

$$= (5 - 20x)\text{kN}$$

Fig. 2.8

i.e. at D, $x = 6$

$$\therefore \quad Q_D = (5 - 20 \times 6)\text{kN}$$

$$= -115\text{kN (downwards)}$$

and at E, $x = 8$

$$\therefore \quad Q_E = (5 - 20 \times 8)\text{kN}$$

$$= -155\text{kN (downwards)}$$

i.e. between D and E the shear force will change uniformly with x, producing a straight line having a slope or gradient of 20 kN/m as shown in fig. 2.9, the SF diagram.

Referring to fig. 2.9, notice how the shape of the SF diagram is affected by the reactions and the loading on the beam. At A the reaction ($R_A = 125\text{kN}$) is acting upwards, causing the shear force to increase from zero to 125 kN. At B,

34

Fig. 2.9

the 80 kN force acting downwards reduces the shear force acting to the right of B from 125 kN to 45 kN. Similarly, at D the 80 kN force acting downwards causes the shear force to change from −35 kN (to the left of D) to −115 kN (to the right of D), while at E the closing vector on the diagram is equal to the reaction R_E (i.e. 155 kN). Between B and D and D and E, the uniformly distributed load of 20 kN/m is illustrated on the SF diagram by the sloping lines MN and OP respectively.

It is important to recognise the effect of the loading on the beam upon the shape of the resulting shear-force diagram.

2.5 Bending moment and bending-moment diagrams

The bending moment at any section of a beam which is in equilibrium is defined as the algebraic sum of the moments of all the external forces acting *either* to the *left* of the section *or* to the *right* of the section being considered (*not both together*),

i.e. $\begin{array}{l}\text{bending moment}\\ \text{at any section}\end{array} = \sum \begin{array}{l}\text{moments of all the external forces acting } \textit{either} \text{ to}\\ \text{the left } \textit{or} \text{ to the right of the section}\end{array}$

The symbol used for bending moment is M.

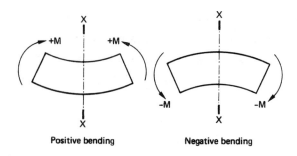

Positive bending   Negative bending

Fig. 2.10 Bending-moment sign convention

When calculating bending moments, the sign convention shown in fig. 2.10 is used. Referring to fig. 2.10,

a) when considering moments to the *left* of XX, clockwise moments are *positive* and anticlockwise moments are *negative*,

b) when considering moments to the *right* of XX, anticlockwise moments are *positive* and clockwise moments are *negative*.

Positive bending causes the beam to 'sag', while negative bending causes the beam to 'hog'. In a 'sagging' beam, the fibres on the top side of the beam are in compression and the fibres on the underside are in tension; while the opposite is the case in a beam which is 'hogging'.

The distribution of bending moment along the length of a beam may be illustrated graphically on a *bending-moment diagram* (BM diagram).

Example For the loaded beam shown in fig. 2.11, calculate the bending moment in sections AB and BC and thus determine the position and magnitude of the maximum bending moment between B and C and the bending moments at A, B, and C respectively. Illustrate the distribution of the bending moment on a BM diagram.

Fig. 2.11

For the purpose of calculating the reactions, the u.d.l. may be replaced by the point load of magnitude 20kN/m x 5m = 100kN shown dotted in fig. 2.11.

36

Taking moments about B,

$$\Sigma \text{ anticlockwise moments} = \Sigma \text{ clockwise moments}$$

$$\therefore \quad 5R_C + 60\text{kN} \times 1\text{m} = 100\text{kN} \times 2.5\text{m}$$

$$\therefore \quad R_C = \frac{(250 - 60)\text{kNm}}{5\text{m}}$$

$$= 38\text{kN}$$

$$\Sigma \text{ upward forces} = \Sigma \text{ downward forces}$$

$$\therefore \quad R_B + 38\text{kN} = (60 + 100)\text{kN}$$

$$\therefore \quad R_B = 122\text{kN}$$

$$M_{XX} = \Sigma \text{ moments of external forces to } \textit{left} \text{ of XX}$$

Consider section AB (fig. 2.12):
For any value of x between 0 and 1 measured from A,

$$M_{XX} = -60\,x \text{ kNm}$$

Fig. 2.12

i.e. at A, $x = 0$

$$\therefore \quad M_A = 0$$

and at B, $x = 1$

$$\therefore \quad M_B = -60 \times 1\text{kNm}$$

$$= -60\text{kNm} \quad \text{(i.e. the beam is 'hogging')}$$

i.e. between A and B the bending moment is changing uniformly with x, producing a straight line having a slope or gradient of -60kNm per metre as shown in fig. 2.14, the BM diagram.

Consider section BC (fig. 2.13):
For any value of x between 1 and 6 measured from A,

$$M_{XX} = [-60\,x + 122(x - 1) - 20(x - 1) \times \tfrac{1}{2}(x - 1)] \text{ kNm}$$

where $20(x - 1)$kN is the total downward force due to the distributed load to the left of any section between B and C which is considered to be a point load acting at distance $\tfrac{1}{2}(x - 1)$m from XX.

37

Fig. 2.13

$\therefore$ M_{XX} = $[-60x + 122x - 122 - 10(x-1)^2]$ kNm

$\qquad$ = $[62x - 122 - 10(x^2 - 2x + 1)]$ kNm

$\qquad$ = $[82x - 10x^2 - 132]$ kNm

which is the equation for a parabola.

At B, $x = 1$

$\therefore$ M_B = $(82 \times 1 - 10 \times 1^2 - 132)$kNm

$\qquad$ = -60kNm $\quad$ (i.e. the beam is 'hogging')

and at C, $x = 6$

$\therefore$ M_C = $(82 \times 6 - 10 \times 6^2 - 132)$kNm

$\qquad$ = 0

The maximum value for M between B and C will occur where $dM_{BC}/dx = 0$.

$$\frac{dM_{BC}}{dx} = 82 - 20x$$

and equating to zero gives

$\qquad$ $0 = 82 - 20x$

$\therefore$ $x = 4.1$

i.e. the bending moment is a maximum value 4.1 m from A.

$\therefore$ $M_{max.}$ = $(82 \times 4.1 - 10 \times 4.1^2 - 132)$kNm

$\qquad$ = 36.1kNm $\quad$ (i.e. the beam is 'sagging')

Plotting values for x at 0.5 intervals between $x = 1$ and $x = 6$ will produce the parabolic curve shown in the bending-moment diagram (fig. 2.14).

Referring to fig. 2.14, notice how the shape of the BM diagram is affected by the loading on the beam. Between A and B, the bending moment is due to the point load at A only and produces a straight line of slope or gradient

38

U.D.L. 20 kN/m

36.1 kNm

BM diagram

Grad. = -60 kNm/m

-60 kNm

4.1 m

Fig. 2.14

−60 kNm per metre; while between B and C, where the load is uniformly distributed, the resulting curve is parabolic.

It is important to recognise the effect of the loading on the beam upon the shape of the resulting bending-moment diagram.

2.6 Relationship between loading, shear-force, and bending-moment diagrams
Figure 2.15 shows the loading, shear-force, and bending-moment diagrams for a beam carrying a point load F at mid-span (fig. 2.15(a)) and for a beam carrying a uniformly distributed load w per metre run over its whole length (fig. 2.15(b)).

Comparing the loading and shear-force diagrams for the beam in fig. 2.15(a)), notice that between A and B and B and C on the beam there is no loading and that, on the shear-force diagram between these points, the *gradient* of the diagram is zero. In the beam shown in fig. 2.15(b), between A and B there is a uniformly distributed load w per metre length acting downwards, and on the shear force diagram between these points the *gradient* of the diagram is $-w$; *i.e. the slope or gradient of the shear-force diagram at any point represents the intensity of the loading on the beam at that point.*

Comparing the shear-force and bending-moment diagrams for both beams, notice the following.

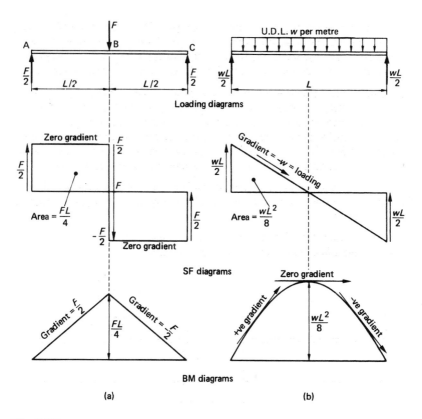

Fig. 2.15

a) The slope or gradient of the bending-moment diagram is *positive* when the shear force is *positive*, and the slope is *negative* when the shear force is *negative*.

b) In fig. 2.15(a), the magnitude of the slope of the bending-moment diagram between A and B is $(FL/4)/(L/2) = F/2$ and between B and C is $(-FL/4)/(L/2) = -F/2$, which represent the values of the shear force between these points; in fig. 2.15(b), at mid-span, the slope of the bending-moment diagram is zero, which is also the magnitude of the shear force at this point — i.e. *the slope or gradient of the bending-moment diagram at any point represents the magnitude of the shear force at that point.*

c) Where the shear force changes sign from positive to negative, the bending moment is a maximum value.

d) The area of the shear-force diagrams to the left of mid-span for each beam is equal to the bending moment at this point; i.e. in fig. 2.15(a) the area of the shear-force diagram to the left of mid-span is $(F/2) \times (L/2) = FL/4$, which is the bending moment at this point, and in fig. 2.15(b) the area to the left

40

of mid-span of the shear-force diagram is $\frac{1}{2}(wL/2) \times (L/2) = wL^2/8$, which is the bending moment at this point — *i.e. the net area of the shear-force diagram to the left (or to the right) of any section represents the bending moment at that section, provided the following sign convention is used:*

i) when considering the area of the shear-force diagram to the *left* of any section XX, the bending moment is *positive* where the net area is *positive* and the bending moment is *negative* where the net area is *negative*,

ii) when considering the area of the shear-force diagram to the *right* of any section XX, the bending moment is *positive* where the net area is *negative* and the bending moment is *negative* where the net area is *positive*.

The relationship between loading, shear-force, and bending-moment diagrams for cantilever beams is shown in fig. 2.16. Referring to fig. 2.16, notice that for both cantilevers

a) the zero datum for XX is the free end of the beam,
b) the SF and BM diagrams are both wholly negative.

Loading diagrams

SF diagrams

BM diagrams

Fig. 2.16

41

Example 1 For the loaded beam shown in fig. 2.17(a), draw the shear-force and bending-moment diagrams, indicating on the BM diagram the position and magnitude of the maximum bending moments.

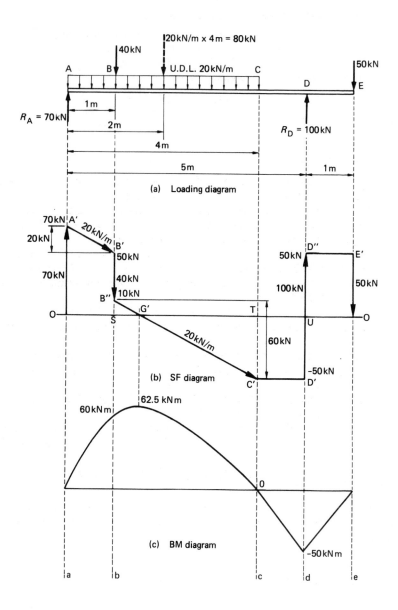

(a) Loading diagram

(b) SF diagram

(c) BM diagram

Fig. 2.17

42

To calculate the reactions, the u.d.l. may be replaced by the point load 20kN/m x 4m = 80kN acting at the mid-point of the u.d.l. and shown dotted in fig. 2.17(a).

Taking moments about A,

$$\Sigma \text{ anticlockwise moments } = \Sigma \text{ clockwise moments}$$

$$\therefore \qquad 5R_D = 40\text{kN} \times 1\text{m} + 80\text{kN} \times 2\text{m} + 50\text{kN} \times 6\text{m}$$

$$\therefore \qquad R_D = 100\text{kN}$$

$$\Sigma \text{ upward forces } = \Sigma \text{ downward forces}$$

$$\therefore \qquad R_A + 100\text{kN} = 40\text{kN} + 80\text{kN} + 50\text{kN}$$

$$\therefore \qquad R_A = 70\text{kN}$$

To draw the shear force diagram:

i) Draw faint and parallel lines Aa, Bb, Cc, Dd, and Ee, vertically downwards from the points A, B, C, D, and E on the loading diagram.
ii) Draw the reference axis OO parallel to the beam in the loading diagram.
iii) From the reference axis, draw line OA' 70 units long and vertically upwards along Aa to represent the vertical reaction R_A.
iv) On the line Bb, fix B' 20 units below A'. Join A'B'. The gradient of A'B' represents the intensity of the loading between A and B (i.e. 20kN/m).
v) From B', draw line B'B" 40 units long and vertically downwards along Bb to represent the vertical downward force at B.
vi) On the line Cc, fix C' 60 units below B". Join B"C'. The gradient of B"C' (i.e. 20kN/m) represents the intensity of the loading on the beam between B and C.
vii) On the line Dd, fix D' by drawing a line parallel to the reference axis from C' to produce C'D'. The gradient of C'D' is zero, which is also the intensity of the loading on the beam between C and D.
viii) From D', draw D'D" 100 units long and vertically upwards along Dd to represent the vertical reaction R_D.
ix) On the line Ee, fix E' by drawing a line parallel to the reference axis from D" to produce D"E'. The gradient of D"E' is zero, which is the intensity of the loading between D and E.
x) Draw E'O along Ee to close the diagram. This line is 50 units long and represents the vertical downward force at E.

Referring to the shear-force diagram (fig. 2.17(b)), the shear force changes sign at G' and D. At these points, the bending moment will have maximum values.

To find the position of G':
On the shear-force diagram, the gradient of the line B"G' is

$$B"G'_{\text{grad.}} = \frac{B"S}{SG'}$$

43

where $B''G'_{grad.} = 20\text{kN/m}$ and $B''S = 10\text{kN}$

$$\therefore \quad SG' = \frac{B''S}{B''G'_{grad.}} = \frac{10\text{kN}}{20\text{kN/m}} = 0.5\text{m}$$

To draw the bending-moment diagram:
Calculate the bending moments at A, B, G', C, D, and E. At any section XX,

M_{XX} = net area of the shear-force diagram to the *left* of XX

$\therefore \quad M_A = 0$ (since there is no shear-force diagram to the left of A)

M_B = area OA'B'S = $\frac{1}{2}(70 + 50)\text{kN} \times 1\text{m}$ = 60kNm (i.e. beam is sagging)

$M_{G'}$ = area OA'B'S + area SB''G'

$\qquad$ = 60kNm + $\frac{1}{2} \times 10\text{kN} \times 0.5\text{m}$

$\qquad$ = 62.5kNm (i.e. beam is sagging)

M_C = area OA'B'S + area SB''G' + area G'TC'

$\qquad$ = 62.5kNm + $\frac{1}{2} \times (-50\text{kN}) \times 2.5\text{m}$

$\qquad$ = 0

M_D = area OA'B'S + area SB''G' + area G'TC' + area TC'D'U

$\qquad$ = 0 + (−50kN) × 1m

$\qquad$ = −50kNm (i.e. beam is hogging)

M_E = area OA'B'S + area SB''G' + area G'TC' + area TC'D'U + area UD''E'O

$\qquad$ = −50kNm + 50kN × 1m

$\qquad$ = 0

Using these calculated values, the bending-moment diagram shown in fig. 2.17(c) has been drawn.

Referring to the bending-moment diagram, notice that at C the bending moment changes sign from positive to negative. This point is known as a *point of contraflexure* or *point of inflexion*. Comparing the shear-force and bending-moment diagrams, where the shear force changes sign from *positive* to *negative* the bending moment has a maximum *positive* value of 62.5kNm, and where the shear force changes sign from *negative* to *positive* the bending moment has a maximum *negative* value of −50kNm.

i.e. the maximum positive bending moment is 62.5kNm and occurs at 1.5m from end A, and the maximum negative bending moment is 50kNm at D.

Example 2 A beam ABCD, 5m long, is simply supported at B, which is 1m from the left-hand end A, and at the other end D. The beam supports point loads of 50kN at end A and 100kN at C, which is 1m from D, together with uniformly distributed loads of 12kN/m between A and B and 20kN/m between

44

U.D.L. 12kN/m
12kN/m × 1m = 12kN
20kN/m × 4m = 80kN
50kN
100kN
A
B   U.D.L. 20kN/m   D
C
0.5
2m
R_B = 141kN
R_D = 101kN
1m
3m
1m

(a)   Loading diagram

B″
79kN
20kN/m
60kN
141kN
19kN
C′
O
S
T
O
50kN
100kN
A′ −50kN
12kN   12kN/m
101kN
−62kN
B′
−81kN C″
20kN   20kN/m
(b)   SF diagram
D′
−101kN

91kNm

G

−56kNm   (c)   BM diagram

Fig. 2.18

45

B and D. Sketch the shear-force and bending-moment diagrams and hence find
the position of the point of contraflexure.

From the information, the loading diagram shown in fig. 2.18(a) has been
drawn. For the purpose of calculating the reactions, the two u.d.l.'s may be
replaced by point loads of magnitude $12\text{kN/m} \times 1\text{m} = 12\text{kN}$ and
$20\text{kN/m} \times 4\text{m} = 80\text{kN}$, each acting at the mid-point of their respective u.d.l.
and shown dotted in fig. 2.18(a).

Taking moments about D,

$$\Sigma \text{ clockwise moments} = \Sigma \text{ anticlockwise moments}$$

$$\therefore \qquad 4R_B = 100\text{kN} \times 1\text{m} + 80\text{kN} \times 2\text{m} + 12\text{kN} \times 4.5\text{m}$$
$$+ 50\text{kN} \times 5\text{m}$$

$$\therefore \qquad R_B = 141\text{kN}$$

$$\Sigma \text{ upward forces} = \Sigma \text{ downward forces}$$

$$\therefore \qquad 141\text{kN} + R_D = 50\text{kN} + 12\text{kN} + 100\text{kN} + 80\text{kN}$$

$$\therefore \qquad R_D = 101\text{kN}$$

Using the method described in the previous example or by calculating the
shear forces at A, B, C, and D, the shear-force diagram shown in fig. 2.18(b)
may be constructed.

To draw the bending-moment diagram:
At any section XX,

$$M_{XX} = \text{net area of shear-force diagram to the } \textit{left} \text{ of XX}$$

$$\therefore \quad M_A = 0$$

$$M_B = \text{area OA}'\text{B}'\text{S}$$

$$= \tfrac{1}{2}[-50 + (-62)] \text{ kN} \times 1\text{m}$$

$$= -56\text{kNm} \quad \text{(i.e. beam is hogging)}$$

$$M_C = \text{area OA}'\text{B}'\text{S} + \text{area SB}''\text{C}'\text{T}$$

$$= -56\text{kNm} + \tfrac{1}{2}(79 + 19)\text{kN} \times 3\text{m}$$

$$= 91\text{kNm} \quad \text{(i.e. beam is sagging)}$$

$$M_D = \text{area OA}'\text{B}'\text{S} + \text{area SB}''\text{C}'\text{T} + \text{area TC}''\text{D}'\text{O}$$

$$= 91\text{kNm} + \tfrac{1}{2}[-81 + (-101)] \text{ kN} \times 1\text{m}$$

$$= 0$$

Using these calculated values, the bending-moment diagram shown in fig.
2.18(c) may be drawn. Referring to the bending-moment diagram, the point
of contraflexure is at G, which is between B and C.

To find the point of contraflexure

Method 1:
Figure 2.19(a) shows part of the loading diagram. At section XX,

$$M_{XX} = [-50x - 12(x - 0.5) + 141(x - 1) - 20(x - 1) \times \tfrac{1}{2}(x - 1)] \text{ kNm}$$
$$= [-10x^2 + 99x - 145] \text{ kNm}$$

(a) Part of loading diagram   (b) Part of SF diagram

Fig. 2.19

At the point of contraflexure G, $M_G = 0$

$\therefore\quad 0 = -10x^2 + 99x - 145$

$\therefore\quad x = \dfrac{-99 \pm \sqrt{[99^2 - 4 \times (-10) \times (-145)]}}{2 \times (-10)}$

$\qquad = \dfrac{-99 \pm 63.25}{-20}$

$\qquad = 1.79 \quad \text{or} \quad 8.11$

i.e. the point of contraflexure is 1.79 m from the left-hand end A.

Method 2
Figure 2.19(b) shows part of the shear-force diagram. At any section XX,

$\qquad M_{XX}$ = net area of shear-force diagram to the *left* of XX

At the point of contraflexure G, $M_G = 0$

$\therefore\quad M_G = $ area OA'B'S + area SB''G'G

47

$$0 = -56\,\mathrm{kNm} + \tfrac{1}{2}[79 + (79 - 20x)] \times x\,\mathrm{kNm}$$

$$= -56 + 79x - 10x^2$$

$$\therefore \quad x = \frac{-79 \pm \sqrt{[79^2 - 4 \times (-10) \times (-56)]}}{2 \times (-10)}$$

$$= \frac{-79 \pm 63.25}{-20}$$

$$= 0.79 \quad \text{or} \quad 7.11$$

i.e. the point of contraflexure is 0.79 m from B, or 1.79 m from the left-hand end A.

2.7 Geometrical properties of plane sections

A *plane section* is one in which the surface lies in one plane. For example, figs 2.20(a) and (b) are plane sections since they are located in the plane, or on the surface, of the paper.

First moment of area

In the plane section shown in fig. 2.20(a), the first moment N of the area of the section about the axis XX is

$$N = \Sigma y\,\delta A$$

where y is the perpendicular distance of the elemental area δA from the axis XX.

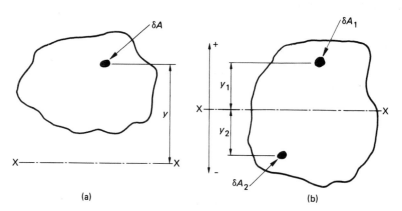

(a)   (b)

Fig. 2.20

In fig. 2.20(b), the first moment of the area *above* the axis XX is

$$N_1 = \Sigma y_1\,\delta A_1$$

the first moment of the area *below* the axis XX is

$$N_2 = \Sigma -y_2\,\delta A_2$$

48

i.e. y measured *below* the axis XX is *negative*
and the *total* first moment of area about the axis XX is

$$N = N_1 - N_2$$

or $\quad N = \Sigma y\ \delta A$

For the special case where the axis XX passes through the centroid G of the section,

$$\Sigma y\ \delta A\ = 0$$

or $\quad N_1 = N_2$

which it is useful to remember.

The units for first moment of area are metres cubed (m^3).

Centroid of area

In any plane area, the centroid G is located at the intersection of all the axes about which the total first moment of area is zero. For example, in the rectangle shown in fig. 2.21, the centroid G is at the intersection of the axes of symmetry XX and YY. About axis XX,

$$N_{XX} = \tfrac{1}{2}d \times b \times \tfrac{1}{4}d + \tfrac{1}{2}d \times b \times (-\tfrac{1}{4}d) = 0$$

and about axis YY,

$$N_{YY} = \tfrac{1}{2}b \times d \times \tfrac{1}{4}b + \tfrac{1}{2}b \times d \times (-\tfrac{1}{4}b) = 0$$

The first moment of area about any other axis (e.g. ZZ) which passes through the centroid G will also be zero.

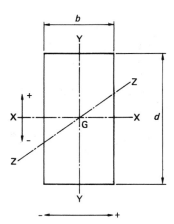

Fig. 2.21

Second moment of area

In the plane section shown in fig. 2.22, the second moment of area I about the axis XX is

49

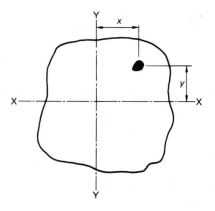

Fig. 2.22

$$I_{XX} = \Sigma y^2 \, \delta A$$

and about axis YY is

$$I_{YY} = \Sigma x^2 \, \delta A$$

which it is useful to remember.

The units for second moment of area are metres to the fourth (m^4).

Second moment of area of common sections
For the *rectangle* shown in fig. 2.23(a), the second moment of area about the axis XX is given by

$$I_{XX} = \frac{bd^3}{12}$$

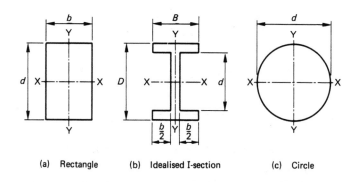

(a) Rectangle   (b) Idealised I-section   (c) Circle

Fig. 2.23

and about axis YY is

$$I_{YY} = \frac{db^3}{12}$$

which should be remembered.

For the *idealised I-section* (fig. 2.23 b)),

$$I_{XX} = \frac{BD^3}{12} - \frac{bd^3}{12} = \frac{1}{12}(BD^3 - bd^3)$$

and $I_{YY} = \dfrac{(D-d)B^3}{12} + \dfrac{d(B-b)^3}{12} = \dfrac{1}{12}\,[(D-d)B^3 + d(B-b)^3]$

which are useful to remember.

For the *circle* (fig. 2.23(c)),

$$I_{XX} = I_{YY} = \frac{\pi d^4}{64}$$

which should be remembered.

2.8 Assumptions made in the simple theory of bending

Figure 2.24 shows a simply supported beam with a transverse force F at mid-span. The beam bends under the force, causing the fibres in the plane of aa to be compressed and the fibres in the plane of bb to be stretched, setting up associated compressive and tensile stresses, called *bending stresses*, in the beam material. At a plane in the beam cross-section known as the *neutral plane* or *neutral axis*, there will be no change in the length of the fibres and thus no bending stress — i.e. the neutral axis is a plane of zero bending stress. It will be shown in section 2.10 that the neutral axis of a beam cross-section passes through the centroid G of the section.

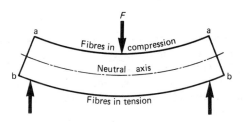

Fig. 2.24

The magnitude and sense of the bending stress at any point in a beam material will depend upon

a) the magnitude and sense of the bending moment at that point,
b) the shape and size of the beam cross-section.

51

In developing the simple theory of bending, it is assumed that

i) the beam cross-section is symmetrical about the axis of loading – fig. 2.25 illustrates a beam cross-section which may be both symmetrically and asymmetrically loaded;

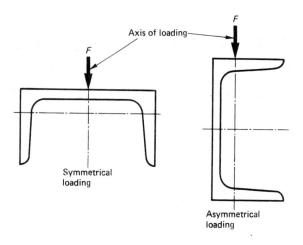

Fig. 2.25

ii) the material of the beam is completely homogeneous, i.e. its molecular structure is the same throughout;

iii) the material of the beam is elastic and, within the elastic limit, obeys Hooke's law – i.e. strain is directly proportional to the stress producing it;

iv) cross-sections which are plane and at right angles to the longitudinal axis *before* bending remain plane and at right angles to the axis *after* bending;

v) the *shape* of the section remains the same before and after bending;

vi) the effect of shear is ignored.

2.9 Distribution of bending stress

If the simply supported beam in fig. 2.26(a) is loaded as shown, it will bend to the shape of fig. 2.26(b), i.e. between the supports the bent shape of the beam is a circular arc of mean radius R. An enlarged view of a small portion of the beam between the supports is shown in figs 2.26(c) and (d).

Before bending (fig. 2.26(c)),

$$AA = BB = CC = DD$$

Consider the planes BB and CC after bending (fig. 2.26(d)). After bending, CC remains unchanged,

i.e. $CC = R\delta\theta$

and BB increases to $B'B' = (R + y)\delta\theta$

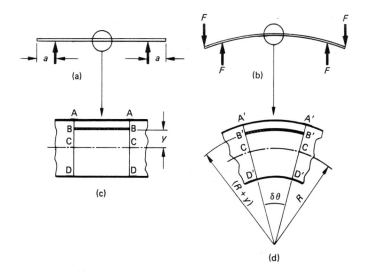

Fig. 2.26 Simply supported beam

∴   increase in length of BB = B′B′ − BB

$$= (R + y)\,\delta\theta - R\delta\theta \quad \text{(since } \mathbf{BB} = \mathbf{CC} = R\delta\theta)$$

$$= y\delta\theta$$

Because the length of BB has been increased, a *strain* is induced in the beam material. From section 1.3,

$$\text{strain} = \frac{\text{change in dimension}}{\text{original dimension}}$$

$$= \frac{y\delta\theta}{R\delta\theta} = \frac{y}{R}$$

From section 1.4,

$$\text{modulus of elasticity } E = \frac{\text{stress }(\sigma)}{\text{strain }(\epsilon)}$$

∴ $\text{strain} = \dfrac{\sigma}{E} = \dfrac{y}{R}$

or $\sigma = \dfrac{E}{R}\,y$

Thus, *the bending stress at any plane in the beam section is directly proportional to the distance* y *from the neutral axis,* which it is useful to remember.

53

Figure 2.27(a) shows the distribution of bending stress across the beam cross-section of fig. 2.27(b). Above the neutral axis (n.a.), the tensile stress increases from zero (at the neutral axis) to σ_t. Below the neutral axis, the compressive stress increases from zero (at the neutral axis) to σ_c.

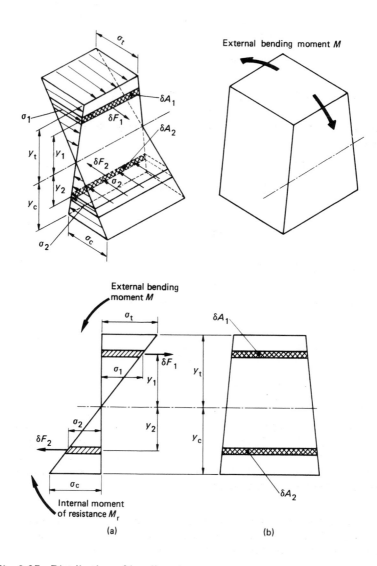

Fig. 2.27 Distribution of bending stress

54

2.10 Position of the neutral axis

Figure 2.27(a) shows the distribution of bending stress across the section of the beam in fig. 2.27(b) due to the external bending moment M. Consider the force δF_1 acting on the area δA_1 at distance y_1 from the neutral axis,

i.e. $\quad \delta F_1 = \sigma_1 \delta A_1$

From fig. 2.27(a),

$$\sigma_1 = \frac{\sigma_t}{y_t} y_1$$

$\therefore \qquad \qquad \delta F_1 = \frac{\sigma_t}{y_t} y_1 \delta A_1$

and $\quad$ total force $F_1 = \Sigma \delta F_1 = \frac{\sigma_t}{y_t} \Sigma y_1 \, \delta A_1$

Also, the force acting on area δA_2 at distance y_2 below the neutral axis is given by

$$\delta F_2 = \sigma_2 \, \delta A_2$$

but $\qquad \sigma_2 = \frac{\sigma_c}{y_c} y_2 = \frac{\sigma_t}{y_t} y_2 \quad \left(\text{since } \frac{\sigma_t}{y_t} = \frac{\sigma_c}{y_c} \right)$

$\therefore \qquad \qquad \delta F_2 = \frac{\sigma_t}{y_t} y_2 \, \delta A_2$

and $\quad$ total force $F_2 = \Sigma \delta F_2 = \frac{\sigma_t}{y_t} \Sigma y_2 \, \delta A_2$

Since the beam is in equilibrium,

$$F_1 = F_2$$

i.e. $\qquad \frac{\delta_t}{y_t} \Sigma y_1 \, \delta A_1 = \frac{\sigma_t}{y_t} \Sigma y_2 \, \delta A_2$

$\therefore \qquad \qquad \Sigma y_1 \, \delta A_1 = \Sigma y_2 \, \delta A_2$

or $\quad \Sigma y_1 \, \delta A_1 - \Sigma y_2 \, \delta A_2 = 0$

i.e. the algebraic sum of the first moments of area about the neutral axis is zero.

By definition, for the algebraic sum of the first moments of area about a point in a plane to be zero, that point must be the centroid of the area; thus, *the neutral axis or axis of zero stress must pass through the centroid of the section*, which should be remembered.

2.11 Relationship between bending stress and external bending moment

Referring to fig. 2.27(a), the forces δF_1 and δF_2 are exerting about the neutral axis a *clockwise* moment of magnitude

$$\delta M_r = \delta F_1 y_1 + \delta F_2 y_2$$

where $\delta F_1 = \dfrac{\sigma_t}{y_t} y_1 \delta A_1$ and $\delta F_2 = \dfrac{\sigma_t}{y_t} y_2 \delta A_2$

$\therefore \quad \delta M_r = \dfrac{\sigma_t}{y_t} y_1 \delta A_1 y_1 + \dfrac{\sigma_t}{y_t} y_2 \delta A_2 y_2$

$\qquad = \dfrac{\sigma_t}{y_t} (y_1{}^2 \delta A_1 + y_2{}^2 \delta A_2)$

$\therefore$ the total clockwise moment about the neutral axis is given by

$\qquad M_r = \Sigma \, \delta M_r$

$\qquad = \dfrac{\sigma_t}{y_t} \Sigma y^2 \, \delta A$

This moment is known as the *internal moment of resistance to bending* and, since the beam is in equilibrium, it is equal in magnitude but opposite in direction to the external bending moment M. Also, from section 2.7, the term $\Sigma y^2 \, \delta A$ is the second moment of area I about the neutral axis of the section,

$\therefore \quad M_r = M = \dfrac{\sigma_t}{y_t} I$

Thus, at *any* distance y from the neutral axis,

$\qquad M = \dfrac{\sigma}{y} I$

or $\quad \sigma = \dfrac{M}{I} y$

From section 2.9,

$\qquad \sigma = \dfrac{E}{R} y$

$\therefore \quad \dfrac{M}{I} = \dfrac{\sigma}{y} = \dfrac{E}{R}$

which is known as the *simple bending equation and should be remembered.*

Example 1 A beam of rectangular cross-section, 40 mm x 160 mm deep, is subjected to a bending moment of 35 kN m. Determine the maximum bending stress in the beam material.

From the simple bending equation,

$\qquad \sigma = My/I$

where $M = 35 \, \text{kN m} = 35 \times 10^3 \, \text{N m}$ $\qquad y = 80 \, \text{mm} = 0.08 \, \text{m}$

and $I = bd^3/12 = 40\,\text{mm} \times (160\,\text{mm})^3/12 = 13.65 \times 10^6\,\text{mm}^4$

$$= 13.65 \times 10^{-6}\,\text{m}^4$$

(notice that, to convert mm^4 to m^4, multiply by 10^{-12})

$$\therefore \quad \sigma = \frac{35 \times 10^3\,\text{Nm} \times 0.08\,\text{m}}{13.65 \times 10^{-6}\,\text{m}^4}$$

$$= 205.1 \times 10^6\,\text{N/m}^2 \quad \text{or} \quad 205.1\,\text{MN/m}^2$$

i.e. the bending stress is $205.1\,\text{MN/m}^2$.

Example 2 The cross-section of the idealised I-beam shown in fig. 2.28 has overall dimensions of 100 mm x 150 mm deep with a flange and web thickness of 20 mm. Calculate the second moment of area of the section about the neutral axis. If the bending stress in the beam material is not to exceed $180\,\text{MN/m}^2$, determine the maximum bending moment in the beam.

Fig. 2.28 Idealised I-beam section

For an idealised I-beam,

$$I_{\text{n.a.}} = \frac{1}{12}(BD^3 - bd^3)$$

where $B = 100\,\text{mm} = 0.1\,\text{m}$ $\quad D = 150\,\text{mm} = 0.15\,\text{m}$
$b = (100 - 20)\,\text{mm} = 0.08\,\text{m}$ and $\quad d = (150 - 40)\,\text{mm} = 0.11\,\text{m}$

$$\therefore \quad I_{\text{n.a.}} = \frac{1}{12}[0.1\,\text{m} \times (0.15\,\text{m})^3 - 0.08\,\text{m} \times (0.11\,\text{m})^3]$$

$$= 1.925 \times 10^{-5}\,\text{m}^4$$

i.e. the second moment of area about the neutral axis is $1.925 \times 10^{-5}\,\text{m}^4$.

From the simple bending equation,

$$M = \sigma I/y$$

where $\sigma = 180\,\text{MN/m}^2 = 180 \times 10^6\,\text{N/m}^2$ $\quad y = 75\,\text{mm} = 0.075\,\text{m}$

and $I = 1.925 \times 10^{-5} \text{ m}^4$

$$\therefore \quad M = \frac{180 \times 10^6 \text{ N/m}^2 \times 1.925 \times 10^{-5} \text{ m}^4}{0.075 \text{ m}}$$

$$= 46.2 \times 10^3 \text{ Nm} \quad \text{or} \quad 46.2 \text{ kNm}$$

i.e. the maximum bending moment is 46.2 kNm.

Example 3 A steel bar, 100 mm diameter, is used to support a pulley block. If the bar is simply supported over a span of 1.2 m, determine the maximum bending stress in the material when the pulley block is at mid-span supporting a load of 20 kN.

Fig. 2.29

The problem is shown diagrammatically in fig. 2.29.

Referring to fig. 2.29, the maximum bending moment occurs at mid-span,

$$\therefore \quad M_{\text{max.}} = \Sigma \text{ moments to } left \text{ of mid-span}$$

$$= 10 \text{ kN} \times 0.6 \text{ m}$$

$$= 6 \text{ kNm} \quad \text{or} \quad 6 \times 10^3 \text{ Nm}$$

$$\sigma_{\text{max.}} = M_{\text{max.}} \, y/I$$

where $y = (100 \text{ mm})/2 = 0.05 \text{ m}$

and $I = \pi d^4/64 = \pi (0.1 \text{ m})^4/64 = 4.91 \times 10^{-6} \text{ m}^4$

$$\therefore \quad \sigma_{\text{max.}} = \frac{6 \times 10^3 \text{ Nm} \times 0.05 \text{ m}}{4.91 \times 10^{-6} \text{ m}^4}$$

$$= 61.1 \times 10^6 \text{ N/m}^2 \quad \text{or} \quad 61.1 \text{ MN/m}^2$$

i.e. the maximum bending stress is 61.1 MN/m².

Example 4 The maximum bending moment and bending stress in a beam of rectangular cross-section must not exceed 25 kNm and 130 MN/m² respectively. What will be the minimum dimensions of the beam cross-section if the width of the beam is two-thirds of its depth?

$$I = bd^3/12 \quad \text{and} \quad b = \tfrac{2}{3}d$$

$$\therefore \quad I = \frac{2}{3} d \times \frac{d^3}{12} = \frac{d^4}{18}$$

From the simple bending equation,

$$\sigma = My/I$$

where
$$\sigma = 130\,\text{MN/m}^2 = 130 \times 10^6\,\text{N/m}^2$$
$$M = 25\,\text{kNm} = 25 \times 10^3\,\text{Nm} \quad \text{and} \quad y = 0.5\,d$$

$$\therefore \quad 130 \times 10^6\,\text{N/m}^2 = \frac{25 \times 10^3\,\text{Nm} \times 0.5\,d}{d^4/18}$$

$$\therefore \quad d^3 = \frac{25 \times 10^3\,\text{Nm} \times 0.5 \times 18}{130 \times 10^6\,\text{N/m}^2}$$

$$= 1.731 \times 10^{-3}\,\text{m}^3$$

$$\therefore \quad d = 0.12\,\text{m} \quad \text{or} \quad 120\,\text{mm}$$

and $b = \frac{2}{3} \times 120\,\text{mm}$

$$= 80\,\text{mm}$$

i.e. the beam dimensions are 80 mm x 120 mm deep.

Example 5 Calculate the maximum force which can be applied at mid-span to the simply supported beam shown in fig. 2.30, if the maximum bending stress at this point is not to exceed $200\,\text{MN/m}^2$.

Fig. 2.30

By inspection of fig. 2.30,

reaction at A = reaction at B

$$= \tfrac{1}{2}[(10\text{kN/m} \times 4\text{m}) + F\,\text{kN}]$$

$$= (20 + \tfrac{1}{2}F)\,\text{kN}$$

At mid-span,

$M = \Sigma$ moments to *left* of mid-span

$$= [(20 + \tfrac{1}{2}F)\,\text{kN} \times 2\text{m}] - [(10\text{kN/m} \times 2\,\text{m}) \times 1\,\text{m}]$$

$$= (20 + F)\,\text{kNm} \quad \text{or} \quad (20 + F) \times 10^3\,\text{Nm}$$

From the simple bending equation,

$$M = \sigma I/y$$

where $\sigma = 200\,\text{MN/m}^2 = 200 \times 10^6\,\text{N/m}^2$

$I = 16 \times 10^6\,\text{mm}^4 = 16 \times 10^{-6}\,\text{m}^4$

and $y = (150\,\text{mm})/2 = 0.075\,\text{m}$

$\therefore \quad (20 + F) \times 10^3\,\text{Nm} = \dfrac{200 \times 10^6\,\text{N/m}^2 \times 16 \times 10^{-6}\,\text{m}^4}{0.075\,\text{m}}$

$$= 42.67 \times 10^3\,\text{N m}$$

$\therefore \qquad\qquad\qquad = 42.67 - 20$

$$= 22.67\,\text{kN}$$

i.e. the maximum force at mid-span is 22.67 kN.

2.12 Section modulus

At any section in a loaded beam, the greatest bending stress occurs in the fibres furthest from the neutral axis of the beam cross-section, i.e. when the value of y is a maximum. Thus, at *any* section,

$$\sigma_{\text{max.}} = \frac{My_{\text{max.}}}{I}$$

The term $I/y_{\text{max.}}$ is known as the *section modulus*, Z, and has units metres cubed (m^3),

$\therefore \quad \sigma_{\text{max.}} = \dfrac{M}{Z}$

which it is useful to remember.

For beams of rectangular cross-section (b wide x d deep),

$$Z = \frac{I}{y_{\text{max.}}}$$

$$= \frac{bd^3/12}{d/2}$$

$$= \frac{bd^2}{6}$$

For circular beams of diameter d,

$$Z = \frac{\pi d^4/64}{d/2}$$

$$= \frac{\pi d^3}{32}$$

Example 1 Calculate the section modulus of a rectangular beam having a cross-section 200 mm wide by 300 mm deep.

$$Z = bd^2/6$$

where $b = 200\,\text{mm} = 0.2\,\text{m}$ and $d = 300\,\text{mm} = 0.3\,\text{m}$

$$\therefore \quad Z = \frac{0.2\,\text{m} \times (0.3\,\text{m})^2}{6}$$

$$= 0.003\,\text{m}^3$$

i.e. the section modulus is $0.003\,\text{m}^3$.

Example 2 What diameter of beam will have the same section modulus as the beam in example 1 above?

For a circular beam,

$$Z = \pi d^3/32$$

$$\therefore \quad d^3 = \frac{32Z}{\pi}$$

$$= \frac{32 \times 0.003\,\text{m}^3}{\pi}$$

$$= 0.0306\,\text{m}^3$$

$$\therefore \quad d = 0.3126\,\text{m} \quad \text{or} \quad 312.6\,\text{mm}$$

i.e. the diameter is 312.6 mm.

Example 3 At a point in a beam having a section modulus of $21.3 \times 10^{-3}\,\text{m}^3$, the bending moment is 40 kNm. What is the maximum bending stress at this point?

$$\sigma_{\text{max.}} = M/Z$$

where $M = 40\,\text{kNm} = 40 \times 10^3\,\text{Nm}$ and $Z = 21.3 \times 10^3\,\text{m}^3$

$$\therefore \quad \sigma_{\text{max.}} = \frac{40 \times 10^3\,\text{Nm}}{21.3 \times 10^{-3}\,\text{m}^3}$$

$$= 1.88 \times 10^6\,\text{N/m}^2 \quad \text{or} \quad 1.88\,\text{MN/m}^2$$

i.e. the maximum bending stress is $1.88\,\text{MN/m}^2$.

2.13 Tables of properties

In general engineering practice, beams are selected from available standard stock sizes for which values of I, Z, etc. are known. A selection of readily available standard beam cross-sections are shown in Tables 2.1, 2.2, and 2.3. The values in these tables, which are abridged, have been reproduced from the *Structural steelwork handbook* by kind permission of the British

Table 2.1 Universal beams (fig. 2.31)

Size $D \times B$ (mm)	Mass per metre (kg)	Thickness		I_{xx} (cm^4)	I_{yy} (cm^4)	Z_{xx} (cm^3)	Z_{yy} (cm^3)
		Web t (mm)	Flange T (mm)				
910.3 x 304.1	222	15.9	23.9	375 924	11 223	8259	738.1
840.7 x 292.4	194	14.7	21.7	279 450	9069	6648	620.4
762.0 x 266.7	173	14.3	21.6	205 177	6846	5385	513.4
677.9 x 253.0	125	11.7	16.2	118 003	4379	3481	346.1
617.5 x 307.0	113	14.1	23.6	151 631	11 412	4911	743.3
533.1 x 209.3	92	10.2	15.6	55 353	2392	2076	228.6
467.4 x 192.8	98	11.4	19.6	45 717	2343	1956	243.0
457.2 x 151.9	67	9.1	15.0	28 577	878	1250	115.5
402.3 x 142.4	46	6.9	11.2	15 647	539	777.8	75.7
364.0 x 173.2	67	9.1	15.7	19 522	1362	1073	157.3
352.8 x 126.0	39	6.5	10.7	10 087	357	571.8	56.6
310.9 x 166.8	54	7.7	13.7	11 710	1061	753.3	127.3
312.7 x 102.4	33	6.6	10.8	6487	193	415.0	37.8
254.0 x 101.6	22	5.8	6.8	2867	120	225.7	23.6
203.2 x 133.4	25	5.8	7.8	2356	310	231.9	46.4

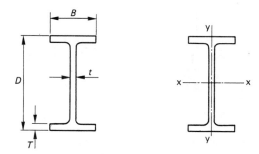

Fig. 2.31 Universal beam

Constructional Steelwork Association Limited and the Constructional Steel Research and Development Organisation.

Example 1 The maximum tensile stress in a universal beam is limited to 80 N/mm^2 when the bending moment is 30 kN·m. From Table 2.1, select a suitable size of beam, ignoring the effect of the mass of the beam itself and assuming the xx axis to be the neutral plane. What will be the actual stress in the chosen beam?

Table 2.2 Structural tees cut from universal beams (fig. 2.32)

Size B × A (mm)	Mass per metre (kg)	Thickness		I_{xx} (cm⁴)	Z_{xx} (cm³)	Extreme fibre distance	
		Web t (mm)	Flange T (mm)			y_f (cm)	y_t (cm)
304.1 x 455.2	112	15.9	23.9	29 036	869.8	12.1	33.42
292.4 x 420.4	97	14.7	21.7	21 381	690.9	11.1	30.94
266.7 x 381.0	87	14.3	21.6	15 495	551.3	9.99	28.11
253.0 x 339.0	63	11.7	16.2	8997	359.5	8.87	25.03
307.0 x 308.7	90	14.1	23.6	8949	369.5	6.65	24.22
209.3 x 266.6	46	10.2	15.6	3905	194.4	6.56	20.10
192.8 x 233.7	49	11.4	19.6	2978	167.2	5.55	17.82
151.9 x 228.6	34	9.1	15.0	2128	126.1	5.99	16.87
142.4 x 201.2	23	6.9	11.2	1130	75.0	5.05	15.07
173.2 x 182.0	34	9.1	15.7	1158	81.6	4.01	14.19
126.0 x 176.4	20	6.5	10.7	719.6	54.4	4.41	13.23
166.8 x 155.4	27	7.7	13.7	636.4	51.5	3.19	12.35
102.4 x 156.3	17	6.6	10.8	486.7	42.4	4.14	11.49
101.6 x 127.0	11	5.8	6.8	227.2	24.7	3.49	9.21
133.4 x 101.6	13	5.8	7.8	133.7	16.6	2.12	8.04

Fig. 2.32 Structural tee cut from universal beam

$Z = M/\sigma_{max.}$

where $M = 30\,\text{kNm} = 30 \times 10^3\,\text{Nm}$

and $\sigma_{max.} = 80\,\text{N/mm}^2 = 80 \times 10^6\,\text{N/m}^2$

$$\therefore\ Z = \frac{30 \times 10^3\,\text{Nm}}{80 \times 10^6\,\text{N/m}^2}$$

$$= 0.375 \times 10^{-3}\,\text{m}^3$$

$$= 375\,\text{cm}^3$$

Table 2.3 Gantry girders (fig. 2.33)

| Size $D \times B$ (mm) | Mass per metre (kg) | Extreme fibre distance | | I_{xx} (cm⁴) | Z_{xx} (cm³) |
		y_1 (cm)	y_2 (cm)		
939 x 432	355	39.20	54.68	644 504	11 797
853 x 432	260	32.92	52.37	384 673	7345
774 x 432	239	29.16	48.26	288 718	5982
700 x 432	218	25.58	44.40	215 582	4856
630 x 432	245	24.11	38.86	206 436	5313
627 x 381	195	23.60	39.14	155 882	3982
622 x 381	180	22.74	39.49	140 490	3558
618 x 305	155	23.53	38.22	120 871	3163
555 x 381	177	20.27	35.23	108 879	3091
550 x 305	151	20.84	34.13	92 644	2715
478 x 305	140	17.77	29.98	64 431	2149
472 x 254	117	18.67	28.50	54 593	1916
465 x 229	93	17.57	28.91	39 916	1381
423 x 305	116	14.67	27.62	40 572	1469
418 x 254	95	15.52	26.23	34 059	1298

Fig. 2.33 Gantry girder

[note that values for Z in the tables are in units centimetres cubed (cm³)]
It should be noted that,

$$1 \text{ cm}^3 = 1 \times 10^{-6} \text{ m}^3$$

In Table 2.1, $Z = 375$ cm³ lies between the Z_{xx} values 225.7 cm³ and 415 cm³. If the smaller value for Z_{xx} is used, the maximum stress will be exceeded,

i.e. $\sigma_{\text{max.}} = M/Z$

$$= \frac{30 \times 10^3 \,\text{Nm}}{225.7 \times 10^{-6} \,\text{m}^3}$$

$$= 132.9 \times 10^6 \,\text{N/m}^2 \quad \text{or} \quad 132.9 \,\text{N/mm}^2$$

therefore, select the beam for which $Z_{xx} = 415 \,\text{cm}^3$;

i.e. the selected beam is 312.7 mm deep x 102.4 mm wide.

Actual stress in chosen beam $= M/Z_{xx}$

$$= \frac{30 \times 10^3 \,\text{Nm}}{415 \times 10^{-6} \,\text{m}^3}$$

$$= 72 \times 10^6 \,\text{N/m}^2 \quad \text{or} \quad 72 \,\text{N/mm}^2$$

i.e. the actual stress in the selected beam is $72 \,\text{N/mm}^2$.

Example 2   A cantilever beam is 2 metres long and is to support a load of 10 kN at its free end. Select a suitable tee-section beam, indicating the correct orientation, to limit the maximum *tensile* stress in the beam material to $57 \,\text{MN/m}^2$. Take into account the mass of the beam.

Fig. 2.34

The loaded beam is shown in fig. 2.34. Let the beam have weight w/m,

i.e. w/m = mass per metre x g

Referring to fig. 2.34, the maximum bending moment will occur at the support,

$\therefore \ M_{\text{max.}} = -10\text{kN} \times 2\text{m} - (w/\text{m} \times 2\text{m}) \times 1\text{m}$

$$= -20 \times 10^3 \,\text{Nm} - 2w \times 1\text{m}$$

The minus sign indicates that the maximum tensile bending stress is in the upper fibres of the beam cross-section and for the remaining calculations may be ignored; i.e. the beam should be loaded with the flange on the underside.

Since the mass of the beam is unknown, it is first necessary to calculate Z considering the bending moment due to the 10 kN force only (i.e. $M = 20 \times 10^3 \,\text{Nm}$).

$$Z = M/\sigma_{max.}$$

and $\quad \sigma_{max.} = 57\ \text{MN/m}^2 = 57 \times 10^6\ \text{N/m}^2$

$\therefore \quad Z = \dfrac{20 \times 10^3\ \text{Nm}}{57 \times 10^6\ \text{N/m}^2}$

$\qquad = 0.351 \times 10^{-3}\ \text{m}^3 \quad$ or $\quad 351\ \text{cm}^3$

From Table 2.2, the nearest larger Z value is $359.5\ \text{cm}^3$, which has a mass per metre of 63 kg;

$\therefore \quad$ maximum bending moment $= 20 \times 10^3\ \text{Nm} + 2 \times 63\ \text{kg} \times 9.81\ \text{m/s}^2 \times 1\ \text{m}$

$$= 21.236 \times 10^3\ \text{Nm}$$

Check if the maximum bending stress has been exceeded:

$$\sigma_{max.} = M/Z$$

$$= \frac{21.236 \times 10^3\ \text{Nm}}{359.5 \times 10^{-6}\ \text{m}^3}$$

$$= 59.1 \times 10^6\ \text{N/m}^2$$

which is larger than the permissible stress.

Repeating the above procedure for a beam where $Z = 369.5\ \text{cm}^3$ will result in a bending stress of $58.9\ \text{MN/m}^2$, which is still too large.

A beam where $Z = 551.3\ \text{cm}^3$ has a mass per metre of 87 kg. Check for maximum stress value:

$$M_{max.} = 20 \times 10^3\ \text{Nm} + 2 \times 87\ \text{kg} \times 9.81\ \text{m/s}^2 \times 1\ \text{m}$$

$$= 21.71 \times 10^3\ \text{Nm}$$

and $\quad \sigma_{max.} = \dfrac{21.71 \times 10^3\ \text{Nm}}{551.3 \times 10^{-6}\ \text{m}^3}$

$$= 39.4 \times 10^6\ \text{N/m}^2$$

which is within the permissible limit.

i.e. the beam selected is 266.7 mm wide x 381 mm deep and is used with the flange on the underside.

Example 3 The maximum bending stress in the simply supported beam shown in fig. 2.35(a) is limited to $120\ \text{N/mm}^2$. Neglecting the mass of the beam itself, select a suitable gantry girder to be used with the larger flange on the upper side. What will be the actual maximum bending stress in the beam section?

To calculate the reactions, the u.d.l. may be replaced by the point load $18\ \text{kN/m} \times 5\ \text{m} = 90\ \text{kN}$ acting at the mid-point of the u.d.l. and shown dotted in fig. 2.35(a).

Taking moments about E,

$\qquad \Sigma$ clockwise moments $= \Sigma$ anticlockwise moments

(a) Loading diagram

(b) SF diagram

Fig. 2.35

$\therefore$ $6R_\text{A} = 90\text{kN} \times 1\text{m} + 90\text{kN} \times 2.5\text{m} + 60\text{kN} \times 7\text{m}$

$\therefore$ $R_\text{A} = 122.5\text{kN}$

Σ upward forces $= \Sigma$ downward forces

$\therefore$ $122.5\text{kN} + R_\text{E} = 90\text{kN} + 90\text{kN} + 60\text{kN}$

$\therefore$ $R_\text{E} = 117.5\text{kN}$

Using the method described in example 1 of section 2.6, the shear-force diagram shown in fig. 2.35(b) has been drawn. Referring to the shear-force diagram, the bending moment will have a maximum value where the shear force changes sign, i.e. at B and F.

67

To find the position of F,

$$\frac{CC'}{C'F} = \text{slope or gradient of line CF}$$

$$\therefore \quad C'F = \frac{CC'}{\text{slope of CF}}$$

where $CC' = 62.5\,\text{kN}$ and   slope of CF = $18\,\text{kN/m}$

$$\therefore \quad C'F = \frac{62.5\,\text{kN}}{18\,\text{kN/m}}$$

$$= 3.472\,\text{m}$$

From section 2.6, the bending moment at any section XX is given by

$$M_{XX} = \text{net area of the shear-force diagram to the left of XX}$$

$$\therefore \qquad M_B = -60\,\text{kN} \times 1\,\text{m} = -60\,\text{kNm} \quad \text{(beam hogging)}$$

and $M_F = -60\,\text{kNm} + 62.5\,\text{kN} \times 1\,\text{m} + \frac{1}{2} \times 62.5\,\text{kN} \times 3.472\,\text{m}$

$$= 111\,\text{kNm} \quad \text{(beam sagging)}$$

i.e. the maximum bending stress will occur at F and, since the beam is sagging, it will be tensile along the bottom surface.

$$Z = M/\sigma_{max.}$$

where $\sigma_{max.} = 120\,\text{N/mm}^2 = 120 \times 10^6\,\text{N/m}^2$

$$\therefore \quad Z = \frac{111 \times 10^3\,\text{Nm}}{120 \times 10^6\,\text{N/m}^2}$$

$$= 925 \times 10^{-6}\,\text{m}^3 \quad \text{or} \quad 925\,\text{cm}^3$$

From Table 2.3, the nearest larger value for Z is $1298\,\text{cm}^3$, therefore the beam selected is 418mm deep x 254mm wide.

The actual maximum bending stress is given by

$$\sigma = \frac{M}{Z}$$

$$= \frac{111 \times 10^3\,\text{Nm}}{1298 \times 10^{-6}\,\text{m}^3}$$

$$= 85.5 \times 10^6\,\text{N/m}^2 \quad \text{or} \quad 85.5\,\text{N/mm}^2$$

i.e. the actual maximum bending stress is $85.5\,\text{N/mm}^2$.

Exercises on chapter 2

1–6 For each of the loaded beams shown in figs 2.36(a) to (f), calculate the reactions and sketch the shear-force and bending-moment diagrams. Find the

Fig. 2.36

69

Fig. 2.37

70

position and magnitude of the maximum bending moment relative to the left-hand support. [1(a) R_1 = 38.57kN; R_2 = 46.23kN; 99.29kNm at 4m. 2(b) R_1 = 125kN; R_2 = 95kN; 225.625kNm at 3.25m. 3(c) R_1 = 176kN; R_2 = 164kN; 390.4kNm at 4.8m. 4(d) R_1 = 72.25kN; R_2 = 82.75kN; 216.38 kNm at 5.11 m. 5(e) R_1 = 144.4kN; R_2 = 115.6 kN; 418.66 kNm at 4.44 m. 6(f) R_1 = 135 kN; R_2 = 145 kN; 262.8 kN m at 4.375 m.]

7-12 For each of the loaded beams shown in figs 2.37(a) to (f), calculate the reactions, sketch the shear-force and bending-moment diagrams, and find, relative to the left-hand end of each beam, the position and magnitude of the maximum positive and negative bending moments and the position of the point of contraflexure. [7(a) R_1 = 93.33kN; R_2 = 26.67kN; 53.34kNm at 6m; −80kNm at 2m; 3.5m. 8(b) R_1 = 98.75kN; R_2 = 151.25kN; 243.8kNm at 4.94m; −30kNm at 8m; 7.747m. 9(c) R_1 = 85kN; R_2 = 135kN; 90.625kNm at 2.25m; −50kNm at 6m; 5.26m. 10(d) R_1 = 72.5kN; R_2 = 197.5kN; 171.95kNm at 4.3125m; −100kNm at 8m; 7.245m. 11(e) R_1 = 132kN; R_2 = 158kN; 184kNm at 2m; −40kNm at 5m; 4.616m. 12(f) R_1 = 98kN; R_2 = 22kN; 24.1kNm at 4.9m; −60kNm at 2m; 3.35m.]

13 A beam ABCDE, 6m long, is simply supported at B and D and carries point loads of 60kN at the left-hand overhanging end A, 80kN at C, and 100kN at the right-hand overhanging end E, together with a uniformly distributed load of 30kN/m between A and C. AB = DE = 1m, and AC = 4m. Calculate the reactions, sketch the shear-force and bending-moment diagrams, and find, relative to end A, the position and magnitude of the maximum positive and negative bending moments and the position of the points of contraflexure. [R_A = 160kN; R_B = 200kN; 6.7kNm at 3.33m; −100kNm at 5m; 2.667m; 4m]

14 A beam 10m long is simply supported over a span of 8m, the supports being equidistant from each end. The beam carries point loads of 80kN on the left-hand end and 120kN on the right-hand end, together with a uniformly distributed load of 20kN/m which extends from the left-hand end to the right-hand support. Calculate the reactions, sketch the shear-force and bending-moment diagrams, and find, relative to the left-hand end, the position and magnitude of the maximum positive and negative bending moments and the position of the points of contraflexure. [176.25kN; 203.75kN; 55.35kNm at 4.8125m; −120kNm at 9m; 2.46m; 7.17m]

15 A beam ABCDE is 4.5m long and is simply supported at A and D. The beam carries point loads of 20 kN and 15 kN at B and E respectively, and a uniformly distributed load of 8 kN/m between A and C. If AB = 0.5 m and BC = CD = 1.5 m, determine the bending moments at A, B, C, D, and E. [M_A = 0; M_B = 11.15 kN m; M_C = 2.55 kN m; M_D = −15 kN m; M_E = 0]

16 A cantilever beam of rectangular cross-section is 2.2m long and carries a point load of 8 kN at its free end. If the beam cross-section is 30 mm x 80 mm deep, determine the maximum bending stress in the material at a section 0.4 m from the support. [450 MN/m^2]

17 Steep strip, 4mm thick, is to be wound on to a 1.6m diameter drum. If the modulus of elasticity for the steel is 200 GN/m^2, determine the bending stress in the material. [499 MN/m^2]

18   A beam, 3 m long, is simply supported at its ends and is to carry a point load of 30 kN at mid-span. If the beam is rectangular in section, with its depth equal to twice its width, determine suitable dimensions to limit the maximum bending stress at mid-span to $80 \, \text{MN/m}^2$.   [75 mm x 150 mm]

19   The cross-section of an idealised I-section beam has overall dimensions 120 mm x 240 mm deep. If the web and flange are both 25 mm thick, determine the second moment of area of the section. If the maximum bending stress is limited to $100 \, \text{MN/m}^2$, determine the maximum load the cross-section can support at mid-span when it is used as a beam 2.5 m long and simply supported at the ends.   [$83.94 \times 10^{-6} \, \text{m}^4$; 112 kN]

20   The flanges in an idealised I-section beam, 150mm x 300mm deep, are 25 mm thick and the web is 20 mm thick. Determine the dimensions of a rectangular-cross-section beam made from the same material, with a depth equal to twice the width, which will support the same maximum bending moment and bending stress. Compare the masses of the two beams.
[238 mm x 119 mm; $\text{mass}_\text{I} = 0.441 \, \text{mass}_\text{rectangle}$]

21   Working from first principles, show that the neutral axis of a beam cross-section which is symmetrical about its axis of loading passes through the centroid of the section.

   A beam cross-section is tee-shaped, the axis of loading being along the axis of the vertical leg. If the horizontal 'cross bar' is 150 mm wide x 15 mm thick, and the vertical leg is 15 mm thick x 180 mm deep, calculate the position of the neutral axis relative to the top of the 'cross bar'.   [60.68 mm]

22   A circular steel bar is used as a cantilever beam to carry a transverse force of 20 kN at a point 1.5 m from the support. Calculate (to the nearest millimetre) the diameter of the bar required to limit the maximum bending stress in the material to $170 \, \text{MN/m}^2$.   [122 mm]

23   Define the term 'section modulus'.

   At a point in a beam with a section modulus of $0.4 \times 10^{-3} \, \text{m}^3$, the bending moment is 12.5 kN m. What is the bending stress?   [$31.25 \, \text{MN/m}^2$]

24   The maximum bending stress and maximum bending moment in a beam cross-section are not to exceed $120 \, \text{MN/m}^2$ and 30 kN m respectively. Calculate the section modulus. If y_max for the section is 160 mm, determine the second moment of area.   [$0.25 \times 10^{-3} \, \text{m}^3$; $40 \times 10^{-6} \, \text{m}^4$]

The following problems may be solved with the aid of the extracts from the tables of properties given in Tables 2.1, 2.2, and 2.3.

25   A universal beam, 254mm deep x 101.6mm wide, is to be used as a simply supported beam with a span of 4 m. If the bending stress at mid-span is restricted to $130 \, \text{N/mm}^2$, what is the maximum load which can be applied to the beam at this point? [28.48 kN]

26   A gantry girder, 550mm deep x 305mm wide, is simply supported over a span of 18 m and carries a uniformly distributed mass of 300 kg per metre length together with point loads of 20 kN and 30 kN at 5 m and 12 m respectively from one support. Calculate the bending moment under each point load and at mid-span, taking into account the mass of the beam itself. Assuming that the maximum bending moment occurs at one of these points, calculate the maximum tensile and compressive bending stresses in the beam material. [M_{20} = 265.9 kN m; M_{30} = 312.5 kN m; M_{ms} = 319 kN m; 117.5 MN/m² (tensile); 71.8 MN/m² (compressive)]

27 A universal beam, ABCD, is simply supported at B and D and carries point loads of 45 kN at A and 60 kN at C. If AB = 1 m, BC = 3 m, and CD = 2 m, calculate the bending moments at A, B, C, and D. Assuming that the maximum bending moment occurs at one of these points, select from Table 2.1 the minimum size of beam which will restrict the maximum stress in the beam material to 120 N/mm². Ignore the mass of the beam itself. [352.8 mm deep x 126 mm wide]

28 A structural tee-section beam is to be used as a cantilever 3 m long *with the flange uppermost.* If the maximum tensile bending stress in the beam material at the support is restricted to 80 N/mm² when the load acting downwards at the free end is 4.5 kN, select the minimum size of beam. Take into account the mass of the beam itself. What will be the maximum compressive stress in the beam material? [166.8 mm wide x 155.4 mm deep; 285 MN/m²]

29 A loaded beam ABCDE is simply supported at B and D and carries point loads of 40 kN, 80 kN, and 60 kN at A, C, and E respectively, together with a uniformly distributed load of 20 kN/m between B and D. AB = DE = 1 m, and BC = CD = 4 m. Find the dimensions of a suitable universal beam to restrict the maximum bending stress in the beam to 140 N/mm². Ignore the mass of the beam itself. [467.4 mm x 192.8 mm]

30 A beam ABCDE, having the cross-section shown in fig. 2.38, is simply supported at the left-hand end A and at D, which is 1 m to the left of E. The beam carries uniformly distributed loads of 60 kN/m between A and B and 20 kN/m between C and D, together with a point load of 30 kN on the overhanging end at E. AB = 3 m, BC = 1 m, CD = 3 m, and DE = 1 m. Calculate the position and magnitude of the maximum bending stress in the beam material, stating whether it is compressive or tensile. [100 N/mm² compressive, 2.5 m from A]

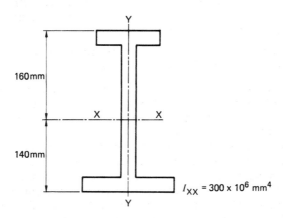

Fig. 2.38

3 Torsion of circular shafts

3.1 Assumptions made in the simple theory of torsion
In developing the simple theory of torsion, it is assumed that

a) the material of the shaft is completely homogeneous, i.e. its molecular structure is the same throughout;
b) the material of the shaft is elastic and, within the elastic limit, obeys Hooke's law;
c) cross-sections which are plane and at right angles to the longitudinal axis of the shaft *before* twisting remain plane and at right angles to the axis *after* twisting;
d) during twisting, the shaft remains circular.

3.2 Shear stress and angle of twist
If a tangential force F is applied at D to the circular shaft of radius r shown in fig. 3.1(a), then a torque of magnitude $T = Fr$ will be applied about B. At the end A, which is rigidly held, there will be an equal and opposite torque acting which can be represented by the tangential force at C as shown in fig. 3.1(b). Since the lines of action of the tangential forces at C and D are separated, these forces are *shearing forces* (see section 1.1) and the angular displacement γ (*gamma*) of the line CD to CE is the *shear strain* at radius r over length l.

Referring to fig. 3.1(b),

$$\text{shear strain } \gamma = \frac{DE}{l} \quad \text{(provided } \gamma \text{ is small)}$$

but $DE = r\theta$

(where θ is measured in radians)

$$\therefore \quad \gamma = \frac{r\theta}{l} \tag{i}$$

i.e. shear strain = radius × twist per unit length
From section 1.10,

$$\text{shear modulus} = \frac{\text{shear stress}}{\text{shear strain}}$$

i.e. $$G = \frac{\tau}{\gamma}$$

74

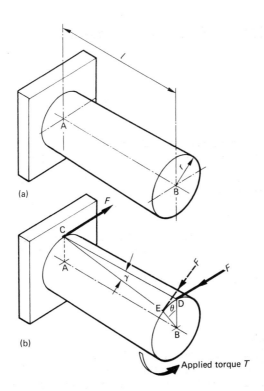

Fig. 3.1 Torsion of a circular shaft

$$\therefore \qquad \gamma = \frac{\tau}{G} \qquad \qquad \text{(ii)}$$

Equating (i) and (ii),

$$\frac{\tau}{G} = \frac{r\theta}{l}$$

or $\quad \dfrac{\tau}{r} = \dfrac{G\theta}{l}$

which should be remembered.

If it is assumed that the shaft remains perfectly circular during twisting and there is no change in the length or diameter, then, after twisting, the radial line BE in fig. 3.1(b) will be perfectly straight, and the *angle of twist* θ between the centre of the shaft, B, and the point on the circumference, E, will be constant — which is a reasonable assumption if the twist per unit length is small (typically 1° in a length equal to 15 diameters) — i.e., for small values of twist per unit length, the term $G\theta/l$ will be constant.

$$\therefore \quad \frac{\tau}{r} = \text{constant}$$

If τ_1, τ_2, and τ_n are the shear stresses at radii r_1, r_2, and r_n etc., then

$$\frac{\tau}{r} = \frac{\tau_1}{r_1} = \frac{\tau_2}{r_2} = \frac{\tau_n}{r_n} = \frac{G\theta}{l}$$

which it is useful to remember.

Example When subjected to an applied torque, a circular shaft of length 600 mm twists through an angle of 2°. If the shear modulus for the shaft material is $80\,\text{GN/m}^2$, determine the shear stress (a) at the centre of the shaft, (b) at a radius of 20 mm.

If the maximum shear stress in the shaft is $120\,\text{MN/m}^2$, what will be the outside diameter?

$$\frac{\tau}{r} = \frac{G\theta}{l}$$

where $G = 80\,\text{GN/m}^2 = 80 \times 10^9\,\text{N/m}^2$ $\theta = 2° = 0.035\,\text{rad}$

and $l = 600\,\text{mm} = 0.6\,\text{m}$

(notice that the angle of twist, θ, must be converted to radians)

$$\therefore \quad \frac{\tau}{r} = \frac{80 \times 10^9\,\text{N/m}^2 \times 0.035\,\text{rad}}{0.6\,\text{m}}$$

$$= 4.67 \times 10^9\,\text{N/m}^3$$

a) At the centre of the shaft, $r = 0$
i.e. the shear stress at the centre of the shaft is zero.

b) When $r = 20\,\text{mm} = 0.02\,\text{m}$,

$$\tau = 4.67 \times 10^9\,\text{N/m}^3 \times 0.02\,\text{m}$$

$$= 93.4 \times 10^6\,\text{N/m}^2 \quad \text{or} \quad 93.4\,\text{MN/m}^2$$

i.e. the shear stress at 20 mm radius is $93.4\,\text{MN/m}^2$.

For a shear stress of $120\,\text{MN/m}^2$,

$$\tau/r = 4.67 \times 10^9\,\text{N/m}^3$$

$$\therefore \quad r = \frac{\tau}{4.67 \times 10^9\,\text{N/m}^3}$$

where $\tau = 120\,\text{MN/m}^2 = 120 \times 10^6\,\text{N/m}^2$

$$\therefore \quad r = \frac{120 \times 10^6\,\text{N/m}^2}{4.67 \times 10^9\,\text{N/m}^3}$$

$$= 25.7 \times 10^{-3}\,\text{m} \quad \text{or} \quad 25.7\,\text{mm}$$

$$\therefore \quad \text{diameter} = 2\,r$$

$$= 2 \times 25.7\,\text{mm}$$

$$= 51.4\,\text{mm}$$

i.e., since the maximum shear stress occurs at maximum radius, the outside diameter of the shaft is 51.4 mm.

3.3 Relationship between shear stress and external torque

Figure 3.2(a) shows the cross-section of a circular shaft subjected to an external torque T, and fig. 3.2(b) illustrates the variation of shear stress across the section. The shear stress varies from zero at the centre to a maximum value at the outside diameter.

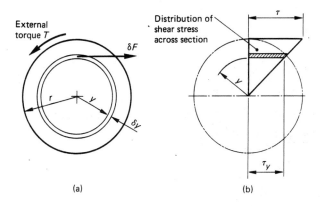

Fig. 3.2   Distribution of shear stress

Referring to fig. 3.2(a), the tangential force δF at radius y due to shear stress τ_y is given by

$$\delta F = \tau_y \times \text{area resisting shear}$$

and   area resisting shear = area of elemental ring

$$= 2\,\pi y\,\delta y$$

$$\therefore \quad \delta F = \tau_y \times 2\,\pi y\,\delta y$$

From fig. 3.2(b),

$$\frac{\tau_y}{y} = \frac{\tau}{r}$$

$$\therefore \quad \tau_y = \frac{\tau y}{r}$$

77

and $\quad \delta F = \dfrac{\tau y}{r} \times 2\pi y\,\delta y$

$$= \dfrac{\tau}{r} \times 2\pi y^2\,\delta y$$

The clockwise moment of this force about the centre of the shaft is given by

$$\delta M_\mathrm{r} = \dfrac{\tau}{r} \times 2\pi y^2\,\delta y \times y$$

$$= \dfrac{\tau}{r} \times 2\pi y^3\,\delta y$$

∴ the total clockwise moment about the centre of the shaft is given by

$$M_\mathrm{r} = \Sigma\,\delta M_\mathrm{r}$$

$$= \dfrac{\tau}{r}\,\Sigma\,2\pi y^3\,\delta y$$

This moment is known as the *internal moment of resistance to torsion*, and, since the shaft is in equilibrium, it is equal in magnitude but opposite in direction to the external torque T.

$$\therefore \quad M_\mathrm{r} = T = \dfrac{\tau}{r}\int_0^r 2\pi y^3\,\mathrm{d}y$$

$$= \dfrac{\tau}{r}\left[\dfrac{2\pi y^4}{4}\right]_0^r$$

$$\therefore \qquad T = \dfrac{\tau}{r} \times \dfrac{\pi r^4}{2}$$

The term $\pi r^4/2$ is known as the *polar second moment of area, J,* about the shaft axis and has units of metres to the fourth (m^4);

i.e. $\quad J = \dfrac{\pi r^4}{2} = \dfrac{\pi d^4}{32} \quad$ (since $d = 2r$)

which should be remembered.

$$\therefore \quad T = \dfrac{\tau}{r}\,J$$

or $\quad \dfrac{T}{J} = \dfrac{\tau}{r}$

From section 3.2,

$$\dfrac{\tau}{r} = \dfrac{G\theta}{T}$$

$$\therefore \quad \frac{T}{J} = \frac{G\theta}{l} = \frac{\tau}{r}$$

which is known as the simple torsion equation and should be remembered.

Example 1   The feed drive shaft on a lathe is 20 mm diameter and is required to transmit a maximum torque of 1 Nm to the apron. Neglecting the effect of the keyway or spline, determine the angle of twist and the maximum shear stress in the drive shaft when the effective driving length is 1.8 m. Take $G = 79\,\text{GN/m}^2$.

From the simple torsion equation,

i.e. $T/J = G\theta/l = \tau/r$

$\qquad \theta = Tl/GJ \quad$ and $\quad \tau = Tr/J$

where $T = 1\,\text{Nm} \qquad l = 1.8\,\text{m} \qquad G = 79\,\text{GN/m}^2 = 79 \times 10^9\,\text{N/m}^2$

$\qquad\qquad r = 10\,\text{mm} = 0{,}01\,\text{m}$

and $J = \pi d^4/32 = \pi \times (0.02\,\text{m})^4/32 = 1.57 \times 10^{-8}\,\text{m}^4$

$\therefore \quad$ angle of twist $\theta = \dfrac{1\,\text{Nm} \times 1.8\,\text{m}}{79 \times 10^9\,\text{N/m}^2 \times 1.57 \times 10^{-8}\,\text{m}^4}$

$\qquad\qquad\qquad\qquad = 1.45 \times 10^{-3}\,\text{rad}$

$\qquad\qquad\qquad\qquad = 0.083° \quad$ or $\quad 5'$

i.e. the angle of twist is 5 minutes.

The maximum shear stress occurs at the maximum radius,

$\therefore \quad \tau_{\text{max.}} = \dfrac{1\,\text{Nm} \times 0.01\,\text{m}}{1.57 \times 10^{-8}\,\text{m}^4}$

$\qquad\qquad\quad = 637 \times 10^3\,\text{N/m}^2 \quad$ or $\quad 637\,\text{kN/m}^2$

i.e. the maximum shear stress is $637\,\text{kN/m}^2$.

Example 2   In a shearing test on a material, failure occurred when the shear stress was $150\,\text{N/mm}^2$. Using a factor of safety of 4, determine the minimum diameter of a shaft made from the material which will transmit a power of 10 kW when rotating at 1500 rev/min. If the shaft is 1.2 m long, what will be the angle of twist? Take $G = 79\,\text{GN/m}^2$.

It is first necessary to determine the torque from the relationship

$\qquad$ power = torque x angular velocity

i.e. $\qquad P = T\omega$

$\therefore \qquad\qquad T = P/\omega$

where $P = 10\,\mathrm{kW} = 10 \times 10^3\,\mathrm{W}$

and $\omega = \dfrac{1500\ \mathrm{rev/min} \times 2\pi\ \mathrm{rad/rev}}{60\ \mathrm{s/min}} = 157.1\ \mathrm{rad/s}$

$\therefore\quad T = \dfrac{10 \times 10^3\,\mathrm{W}}{157.1\ \mathrm{rad/s}} = 63.65\,\mathrm{Nm}$

From the simple torsion equation,

i.e. $T/J = G\theta/l = \tau/r$

$\qquad T/\tau = J/r$

where $\tau = \dfrac{\text{shear stress at failure}}{\text{factor of safety}} = \dfrac{150\,\mathrm{N/mm^2}}{4} = 37.5 \times 10^6\,\mathrm{N/m^2}$

$\qquad J = \pi d^4/32 \quad$ and $\quad r = d/2$

$\therefore\quad \dfrac{63.65\,\mathrm{Nm}}{37.5 \times 10^6\,\mathrm{N/m^2}} = \dfrac{\pi d^4/32}{d/2} = \dfrac{\pi d^3}{16}$

$\therefore\quad d^3 = \dfrac{63.65\,\mathrm{Nm} \times 16}{37.5 \times 10^6\,\mathrm{N/m^2} \times \pi}$

$\qquad\quad = 8.64 \times 10^{-6}\,\mathrm{m^3}$

$\therefore\quad d = 0.0205\,\mathrm{m} \quad$ or $\quad 20.5\,\mathrm{mm}$

i.e. the minimum shaft diameter is 20.5 mm.

For this shaft diameter and maximum shear stress,

$\qquad$ angle of twist $\theta = \tau l/rG$

where $l = 1.2\,\mathrm{m} \qquad G = 79\,\mathrm{GN/m^2} = 79 \times 10^9\,\mathrm{N/m^2}$

and $r = (0.0205\,\mathrm{m})/2 = 0.010\,25\,\mathrm{m}$

$\therefore\quad \theta = \dfrac{37.5 \times 10^6\,\mathrm{N/m^2} \times 1.2\,\mathrm{m}}{0.010\,25\,\mathrm{m} \times 79 \times 10^9\,\mathrm{N/m^2}}$

$\qquad\quad = 0.056\,\mathrm{rad}$

$\qquad\quad = 3.21°$

i.e. the angle of twist in a length of 1.2 m is 3.21°.

3.4 Torsion of hollow circular shafts

Figure 3.3(a) shows the cross-section of a hollow circular shaft subjected to an external torque T, and fig. 3.3(b) illustrates the distribution of shear stress across the section. The shear stress varies from a minimum at the bore to a maximum value at the outside diameter.

From section 3.3, the total internal moment of resistance to torsion across the section is given by

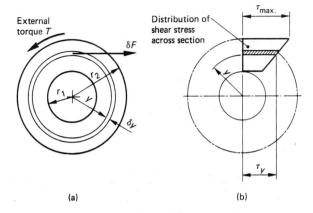

Fig. 3.3 Distribution of shear stress in a hollow shaft

$$M_r = T = \frac{\tau}{r} \Sigma\, 2\pi y^3\, \delta y$$

and, for the section shown in fig. 3.3(a),

$$T = \frac{\tau}{r} \int_{r_1}^{r_2} 2\pi y^3\, dy$$

$$= \frac{\tau}{r} \times \frac{\pi}{2}\, (r_2^4 - r_1^4)$$

The term $(\pi/2)\, (r_2^4 - r_1^4)$ is the polar second moment of area, J, for a hollow section; i.e., for a hollow shaft,

$$J = \frac{\pi}{2}\, (r_2^4 - r_1^4) = \frac{\pi}{32}\, (d_2^4 - d_1^4)$$

which should be remembered.

$$\therefore \quad T = \frac{\tau}{r}\, J$$

or $\dfrac{T}{J} = \dfrac{\tau}{r}$

From section 3.2,

$$\frac{\tau}{r} = \frac{G\theta}{l}$$

$$\therefore \quad \frac{T}{J} = \frac{G\theta}{l} = \frac{\tau}{r}$$

which is the simple torsion equation.

81

Example 1 A hollow shaft of external diameter 50 mm and bore 35 mm is to transmit a torque of 70 Nm. If the shaft is 0.8 m long and the shear modulus is $80\,GN/m^2$, determine (a) the maximum shear stress, (b) the maximum angle of twist.

From the simple torsion equation,

i.e. $T/J = G\theta/l = \tau/r$

$\quad\quad \tau = Tr/J \quad$ and $\quad \theta = Tl/JG$

where $\quad T = 70\,Nm \quad\quad l = 0.8\,m \quad\quad G = 80\,GN/m^2 = 80 \times 10^9\,N/m^2$

and $\quad J = \frac{\pi}{32}\,(d_2^4 - d_1^4) = \frac{\pi}{32}\,[(0.05\,m)^4 - (0.035\,m)^4] = 4.66 \times 10^{-7}\,m^4$

a) The maximum shear stress occurs at the outside diameter, i.e. when $r = 0.025\,m$,

$\therefore \quad \tau_{max.} = \dfrac{70\,Nm \times 0.025\,m}{4.66 \times 10^{-7}\,m^4}$

$\quad\quad\quad = 3.76 \times 10^6\,N/m^2 \quad$ or $\quad 3.76\,MN/m^2$

i.e. the maximum shear stress is $3.76\,MN/m^2$.

b) Angle of twist $\theta = Tl/JG$

$\quad\quad\quad = \dfrac{70\,Nm \times 0.8\,m}{4.66 \times 10^{-7}\,m^4 \times 80 \times 10^9\,N/m^2}$

$\quad\quad\quad = 0.0015\,rad$

$\quad\quad\quad = 0.086° \quad$ or $\quad 5.2'$

i.e. the maximum angle of twist is 5.2 minutes.

Example 2 The hollow shaft in example 1 is to be replaced by a solid circular shaft of equal length and made from the same material. If for an applied torque of 70 Nm the maximum shear stress and angle of twist are not to exceed the values found for the hollow shaft, calculate the minimum solid-shaft diameter. Compare the masses of the two shafts.

From the simple torsion equation,

i.e. $T/J = G\theta/l = \tau/r$

$\quad\quad T/\tau = J/r \quad$ and $\quad J = Tl/G\theta$

Thus, if the solid and hollow shafts are made from the same material and are subjected to the same torque which produces identical values for shear stress and angle of twist, then

$$\frac{J_s}{r_s}\text{ (solid shaft)} = \frac{J_h}{r_h}\text{ (hollow shaft)} \quad\quad\quad\quad\text{(i)}$$

and J_s (solid shaft) = J_h (hollow shaft)   (ii)

Consider equation (i):

for the hollow shaft, $J_h = 4.66 \times 10^{-7}\,\text{m}^4$ and $r_h = 0.025\,\text{m}$

$\therefore$ $\dfrac{J_h}{r_h} = \dfrac{4.66 \times 10^{-7}\,\text{m}^4}{0.025\,\text{m}} = 1.864 \times 10^{-5}\,\text{m}^3$

for the solid shaft, $J_s = \pi d_s{}^4/32$ and $r_s = d_s/2$

$\therefore$ $\dfrac{J_s}{r_s} = \dfrac{\pi d_s{}^4/32}{d_s/2} = \dfrac{\pi d_s{}^3}{16}$

$\therefore$ $\pi d_s{}^3/16 = 1.864 \times 10^{-5}\,\text{m}^3$

$\therefore$ $d_s{}^3 = 9.5 \times 10^{-5}\,\text{m}^3$

$\therefore$ $d_s = 0.0456\,\text{m}$ or   45.6 mm

Consider equation (ii):

for the solid shaft, $J_s = \pi d_s{}^4/32$

$\therefore$ $\pi d_s{}^4/32 = 4.66 \times 10^{-7}\,\text{m}^4$

$\therefore$ $d_s{}^4 = 4.75 \times 10^{-6}\,\text{m}^4$

$\therefore$ $d_s = 0.0467\,\text{m}$ or   46.7 mm

i.e. the minimum diameter of shaft which will satisfy *all* conditions is 46.7 mm.

Let m_s and m_h be the masses of the solid and hollow shafts respectively,

then $\dfrac{m_s}{m_h} = \dfrac{\text{density} \times \text{volume of solid shaft}}{\text{density} \times \text{volume of hollow shaft}}$

Since the shafts are made from the same material and are of equal length,

$\dfrac{m_s}{m_h} = \dfrac{(\pi/4)\,(0.0467\,\text{m})^2}{(\pi/4)\,(0.05^2 - 0.035^2)\,\text{m}^2}$

$= 1.71$

or $m_s = 1.71\,m_h$

i.e. the mass of the solid shaft is 1.71 times greater than the mass of the hollow shaft. Thus, where the *mass* of the shaft is important, hollow shafts are used. For this reason, the propshaft in a front-engined, rear-wheel-drive motor vehicle is hollow.

Example 3   A hollow steel shaft is required to transmit 3000 kW when rotating at 120 rev/min. If the ratio of internal to external diameter is 1:3 and the shear stress is limited to 60 MN/m², determine the required diameters and the twist per unit length. For steel, $G = 79\,\text{GN/m}^2$.

Power $P = T\omega$

$\therefore \qquad T = P/\omega$

where $\quad P = 3000\,\text{kW} \quad$ and $\quad \omega = \dfrac{120\ \text{rev/min} \times 2\,\pi\ \text{rad/rev}}{60\ \text{s/min}} = 12.57\ \text{rad/s}$

$\therefore \quad T = \dfrac{3000\,\text{kW}}{12.57\ \text{rad/s}}$

$\qquad = 238.7\,\text{kNm}$

$\qquad = 238.7 \times 10^3\,\text{Nm}$

From the simple torsion equation,

i.e. $\quad T/J = G\theta/l = \tau/r$

$\qquad J/r = T/\tau$

Let $\quad d_1$ = internal diameter $\quad$ and $\quad d_2$ = external diameter

then $\quad d_2 = 3d_1$

thus $\quad J = (\pi/32) \times [d_2^4 - d_1^4] = (\pi/32) \times [(3d_1)^4 - d_1^4] = 7.85d_1^4$

$\qquad r = d_2/2 = 3d_1/2 \quad$ and $\quad \tau = 60\,\text{MN/m}^2 = 60 \times 10^6\,\text{N/m}^2$

$\therefore \quad \dfrac{7.85d_1^4}{(3d_1/2)} = \dfrac{238.7 \times 10^3\,\text{Nm}}{60 \times 10^6\,\text{N/m}^2} = 3.98 \times 10^{-3}\,\text{m}^3$

$\therefore \qquad d_1^3 = \dfrac{3.98 \times 10^{-3}\,\text{m}^3 \times 3}{7.85 \times 2}$

$\qquad\qquad = 7.6 \times 10^{-4}\,\text{m}^3$

$\therefore \qquad d_1 = 0.0913\,\text{m} \quad$ or $\quad 91.3\,\text{mm}$

and $\qquad d_2 = 91.3\,\text{mm} \times 3$

$\qquad\qquad = 273.9\,\text{mm}$

i.e. the internal and external diameters are 91.3 mm and 273.9 mm respectively.

Now, $\quad \theta/l = \tau/Gr$

where $\quad G = 79\,\text{GN/m}^2 = 79 \times 10^9\,\text{N/m}^2$

and $\qquad r = (0.2739\,\text{m})/2 = 0.137\,\text{m}$

$\therefore \quad \dfrac{\theta}{l} = \dfrac{60 \times 10^6\,\text{N/m}^2}{79 \times 10^9\,\text{N/m}^2 \times 0.137\,\text{m}}$

$\qquad = 5.54 \times 10^{-3}\,\text{rad/m}$

$\qquad = 0.317^\circ/\text{m} \quad$ or $\quad 19\ \text{minutes/m}$

i.e. the angle of twist per unit length is 19 minutes/m.

Exercises on chapter 3

1 A solid circular shaft is 50 mm diameter and 2 m long. Determine the maximum shear stress and angle of twist when the shaft is subjected to an applied torque of 85 Nm. Take G as $80\,GN/m^2$. $[3.46\,MN/m^2;\,11.9']$

2 A solid circular shaft is required to transmit 15 kW when rotating at 3000 rev/min. If the twist per unit length and the maximum shear stress are not to exceed 1.5 degrees/metre and $50\,MN/m^2$ respectively, determine the minimum diameter of shaft required. $G = 80\,GN/m^2$.   [21.9 mm]

3 Working from first principles, develop the simple torsion equation.

A shaft, 100 mm diameter and 470 mm long, transmits 4 kW when rotating at 1500 rev/min. If the shear modulus is $60\,kN/mm^2$, determine the maximum shear stress and angle of twist in the shaft material.
$[130\,kN/m^2;\,4.2'']$

4 The torque on a rotating shaft was determined by measuring the angle of twist. If the diameter of the shaft under test was 70 mm and the twist per unit length was 0.5 degrees/metre, determine the applied torque. What power is the shaft transmitting if it is rotating at 600 rev/min? Take $G = 78\,GN/m^2$.
[1.6 kNm; 100.5 kW]

5 The maximum shear stress and angle of twist in a shaft material are not to exceed $40\,N/mm^2$ and $2°$ respectively. If the diameter of the shaft is 45 mm and the shear modulus is $79\,kN/mm^2$, determine the maximum length of the shaft. How much power will the shaft transmit when it is rotating at 900 rev/min?   [1.551 m; 67.45 kW]

6 A hollow shaft of internal and external diameters 50 mm and 80 mm respectively is 2 m long. If the maximum shear stress in the shaft material is not to exceed $55\,MN/m^2$, determine the power the shaft will transmit when it is rotating at 2000 rev/min. What will be the angle of twist?
Take $G = 80\,GN/m^2$. $[981\,kW;\,1.97°]$

7 A hollow shaft having an external to internal diameter ratio of 2:1 is subjected to a torque of 1500 Nm. If the maximum shear stress in the shaft material is not to exceed $70\,MN/m^2$, determine the shaft dimensions.
[O/D 48.8 mm; bore 24.4 mm]

8 If the shaft in question 7 is replaced by a solid shaft having the same external diameter and equal length, determine (a) the maximum shear stress when the solid shaft is subjected to a torque of 1500 Nm, (b) the percentage increase in the mass of the shaft. $[65.7\,MN/m^2;\,33\%]$

9 The maximum shear stress in a hollow shaft is not to exceed $60\,MN/m^2$. If the ratio of internal to external diameter is 1:2, show that the external diameter is given by

$$D = \sqrt[3]{\frac{P}{1156N}}\ \text{metres}$$

where P = power measured in kilowatts and N = shaft speed in rev/min.

Determine the dimensions of such a shaft to transmit 9000 kW at 600 rev/min, and find the angle of twist per unit length.
Take $G = 80\,GN/m^2$.   [235 mm; 117.5 mm; 22 min/m]

10 Why is it advantageous to use a hollow shaft instead of a solid shaft to transmit power?

A solid shaft, 80 mm diameter, is to be replaced by a hollow shaft made from the same material and of equal length. If the external diameter of the hollow shaft is 100 mm and the maximum shear stress in both shafts is to remain the same for the same applied torque, calculate the diameter of the bore. For the two shafts, compare (a) the masses, (b) the angles of twist. [83.6 mm; m_s/m_h = 2.13; θ_s/θ_h = 1.25]

11   A solid circular shaft of diameter 20 mm and length 375 mm is used as a torsion indicator by measuring the angle of twist. If the maximum angle of twist for an applied torque T is 1.5°, find the magnitude of T. To increase the sensitivity of the device so that for the same applied torque T the angle of twist is 3°, the shaft is replaced by a hollow shaft made from the same material and having the same external dimensions. What will be the bore size? G = 60 GN/m². [65.8 Nm; 16.8 mm]

12   A hollow shaft with external diameter 100 mm and bore 60 mm is 1.6 m long. If the maximum shear stress and angle of twist are not to exceed 60 N/mm² and 2° respectively, determine the maximum speed of rotation of the shaft when transmitting 900 kW. Take G = 80 kN/mm². [838 rev/min]

13   The following results were obtained from a torsion test on a metallic sample of diameter 6 mm using a torsion meter with a gauge length of 50 mm:

Applied torque (Nm)	2	4	6	8	10	12	14	16	18
Angle of twist (rad)	0.013	0.025	0.039	0.053	0.066	0.078	0.092	0.112	0.130

Plot a graph of torque against angle of twist and use it to determine the shear modulus for the material.   [60 GN/m²]

14   The angle of twist in a shaft is restricted to one degree in a length equal to twenty diameters. If the shear modulus in such a shaft is 80 GN/m², determine the shear stress.   [34.9 MN/m²]

15   A hollow shaft with a ratio of outside diameter to bore of 4:3 is to transmit a mean power of 100 kW while rotating at 400 rev/min. If the maximum torque is 1.36 times the mean torque and the shear stress is not to exceed 80 N/mm², determine the dimensions of the shaft.
[67.12 mm x 50.34 mm]

16   Determine the maximum shear stress in a steel propeller shaft, 400 mm external diameter and 200 mm internal diameter, when subjected to a torque of 450 kNm. If the shear modulus of steel is 80 kN/mm², find the angle of twist in a length equal to 20 times the external diameter. Determine the diameter of a replacement solid shaft manufactured from the same material and subjected to the same maximum shear stress.
[38.2 N/mm²; 1.09°; 391.5 mm]

4 Angular motion

4.1 Equations of uniform angular motion
Referring to the graph of angular velocity against time shown in fig. 4.1,

ω_1 = initial angular velocity, with units radians per second (rad/s);

ω_2 = final angular velocity, with units rad/s;

α = uniform or constant angular acceleration, with units rad/s^2

and t = time, with units seconds (s).

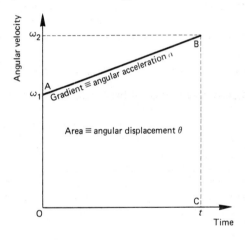

Fig. 4.1 Graph of angular velocity against time

Angular displacement $\theta \equiv$ area OABC

i.e.
$$\theta = \tfrac{1}{2}(\omega_2 + \omega_1)t \qquad \text{(i)}$$

and angular acceleration $\alpha \equiv$ gradient or slope of line AB

i.e.
$$\alpha = \frac{\omega_2 - \omega_1}{t} \qquad \text{(ii)}$$

Multiplying equation (i) by equation (ii) gives

$$\alpha\theta = \tfrac{1}{2}(\omega_2 + \omega_1)t \times \frac{\omega_2 - \omega_1}{t}$$

or $\quad 2\alpha\theta = \omega_2^2 - \omega_1^2$ $\qquad\qquad\qquad\qquad\qquad$ (iii)

From equation (ii),

$\qquad \omega_2 = \omega_1 + \alpha t$ $\qquad\qquad\qquad\qquad\qquad\qquad$ (iv)

Substituting for ω_2 in equation (i),

$\qquad \theta = \frac{1}{2}(\omega_1 + \alpha t + \omega_1)\,t$

or $\qquad \theta = \omega_1 t + \frac{1}{2}\alpha t^2$ $\qquad\qquad\qquad\qquad\qquad$ (v)

Equations (i), (iii), (iv), and (v) above are usually rearranged as follows:

$\qquad \theta = \frac{1}{2}(\omega_2 + \omega_1)t$

$\qquad \theta = \omega_1 t + \frac{1}{2}\alpha t^2$

$\qquad \omega_2 = \omega_1 + \alpha t$

$\qquad \omega_2^2 = \omega_1^2 + 2\alpha\theta$

These equations are known as the equations of uniform angular motion and should be remembered.

Example 1   A flywheel rotating at 210 rev/min is accelerated uniformly for 4 seconds until its speed is 560 rev/min. Determine the uniform angular acceleration and the number of revolutions made by the flywheel in the 4-second period.

From the equations of uniform angular motion,

$\qquad \omega_2 = \omega_1 + \alpha t$

$\therefore \qquad \alpha = (\omega_2 - \omega_1)/t$

and $\qquad \theta = \frac{1}{2}(\omega_2 + \omega_1)t$

where $\quad \omega_1 = \dfrac{210 \text{ rev/min} \times 2\pi \text{ rad/rev}}{60 \text{ s/min}} = 22 \text{ rad/s}$

$\qquad\qquad \omega_2 = \dfrac{560 \text{ rev/min} \times 2\pi \text{ rad/rev}}{60 \text{ s/min}} = 58.6 \text{ rad/s}$

and $\qquad t = 4\,\text{s}$

$\therefore \quad \alpha = \dfrac{58.6 \text{ rad/s} - 22 \text{ rad/s}}{4\,\text{s}}$

$\qquad\quad = 9.15 \text{ rad/s}^2$

i.e. the angular acceleration is 9.15 rad/s^2

$\qquad \theta = \frac{1}{2}(58.6 \text{ rad/s} + 22 \text{ rad/s}) \times 4\,\text{s}$

$\qquad\quad = 161.2 \text{ rad}$

$$\therefore \quad \text{number of revolutions} = \frac{161.2 \text{ rad}}{2\pi \text{ rad/rev}}$$

$$= 25.7$$

i.e. the number of revolutions made by the flywheel in 4 seconds is 25.7.

Example 2   A flywheel is accelerated uniformly from rest for 3 seconds until it is rotating at 210 rev/min. It revolves at 210 rev/min for 4 minutes and is then decelerated uniformly at the rate of 5 rad/s² to rest. For the flywheel, determine (a) the uniform angular acceleration, (b) the deceleration time, (c) the total number of complete revolutions made.

Fig. 4.2

Figure 4.2 illustrates the problem graphically.

a) From the equations of uniform angular motion,

$$\alpha_1 = (\omega_2 - \omega_1)/t_1$$

where $\omega_1 = 0$ (since the flywheel is initially at rest)

$$\omega_2 = \frac{210 \text{ rev/min} \times 2\pi \text{ rad/rev}}{60 \text{ s/min}} = 22 \text{ rad/s}$$

and $t_1 = 3 \text{ s}$

$$\therefore \quad \alpha_1 = \frac{22 \text{ rad/s} - 0}{3 \text{ s}}$$

$$= 7.33 \text{ rad/s}^2$$

Alternatively, from the graph in fig. 4.2,

α_1 = slope of line OB

$$= \frac{22 \text{ rad/s}}{3 \text{ s}}$$

$$= 7.33 \text{ rad/s}^2$$

i.e. the uniform angular acceleration is 7.33 rad/s^2.

b) For the third phase,

$$\omega_2 = \omega_3 + \alpha_3 t_3$$

$\therefore \quad t_3 = (\omega_3 - \omega_2)/\alpha_3$

where $\omega_3 = \omega_1 = 0$ (since the flywheel is brought to rest)

$\omega_2 = 22 \text{ rad/s}$ and $\alpha_3 = -5 \text{ rad/s}^2$ (the minus sign indicating that the flywheel is decelerating or retarding)

$\therefore \quad t_3 = \dfrac{0 - 22 \text{ rad/s}}{-5 \text{ rad/s}} = 4.4 \text{ s}$

Alternatively, from the graph in fig. 4.2,

$$t_3 = \frac{22 \text{ rad/s}}{5 \text{ rad/s}} = 4.4 \text{ s}$$

i.e. the deceleration or retardation time is 4.4 s.

c) | Total angular displacement | = | displacement at constant acceleration | + | displacement at constant velocity | + | displacement at constant retardation |

i.e. $\theta = \theta_1 + \theta_2 + \theta_3$

$$= \tfrac{1}{2}(\omega_2 + \omega_1)t_1 + \omega_2 t_2 + \tfrac{1}{2}(\omega_3 + \omega_2)t_3$$

where $t_2 = 4 \text{ minutes} = 240 \text{ s}$

$\therefore \quad \theta = [\tfrac{1}{2}(22 \text{ rad/s} + 0) \times 3 \text{ s}] + [22 \text{ rad/s} \times 240 \text{ s}]$

$\qquad + [\tfrac{1}{2}(0 + 22 \text{ rad/s}) \times 4.4 \text{ s}]$

$\qquad = 33 \text{ rad} + 5280 \text{ rad} + 48.4$

$\qquad = 5361.4 \text{ rad}$

Alternatively, from the graph in fig. 4.2,

total angular displacement = area OABC

$$= \tfrac{1}{2}(3 \text{ s} + 2 \times 240 \text{ s} + 4.4 \text{ s}) \times 22 \text{ rad/s}$$

$$= 5362.5 \text{ rad}$$

$$\text{Total revolutions made by the flywheel} = \frac{5361.4 \text{ rad}}{2\,\pi \text{ rad/rev}}$$

$$= 853.3$$

i.e. the total number of *complete* revolutions made by the flywheel is 853.

4.2 Torque and angular acceleration

The elemental mass δm at radius r in the disc shown in fig. 4.3 has an angular velocity ω and angular acceleration α. At the instant shown, it also has a *tangential* or *linear* acceleration a.

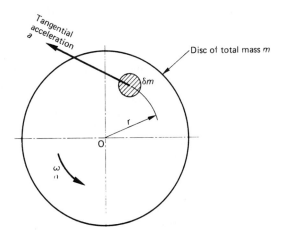

Fig. 4.3   Rotating disc

From Newton's second law of motion, the force acting on δm to produce the acceleration a is given by

$$\delta F = \delta m a$$

and the torque about the centre of rotation O is given by

$$\delta T = \delta F r$$

or $\delta T = \delta m a r$ (vi)

From the relationship between linear and angular motion,

$$a = r\alpha$$

Substituting for a in equation (vi) gives

$$\delta T = \delta m \,(r\alpha)\, r$$

$$= \delta m \, r^2 \alpha$$

91

The total torque to accelerate the complete disc is given by

$$T = \Sigma \delta T$$

$$= \Sigma \delta m\, r^2 \alpha$$

The term $\Sigma \delta m\, r^2$ is called the *mass moment of inertia* or simply the *moment of inertia*, I, of the body about its centre of rotation,

i.e.   torque = moment of inertia x angular acceleration

or $T = I\alpha$

which should be remembered.

The units for moment of inertia are kilogram metre squared (kg m^2).

4.3 Radius of gyration

It is often convenient to consider the total mass of a rotating body as being concentrated at a fixed distance from the axis of rotation; this may be done provided the moment of inertia of the body about that axis remains the same.

The *radius of gyration*, k, of a rotating body is defined as the distance from the axis of rotation at which the total mass m of the body may be considered to be concentrated so that the moment of inertia I of the body about that axis remains the same,

i.e. $I = mk^2$

which should be remembered.

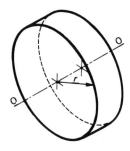

Fig. 4.4

For the solid disc shown in fig. 4.4, the radius of gyration about the axis OO is

$$k = \frac{r}{\sqrt{2}} = \frac{d}{2\sqrt{2}}$$

or $k^2 = \dfrac{r^2}{2} = \dfrac{d^2}{8}$

which it is useful to remember.

Thus, if the total mass of the solid disc in fig. 4.4 is concentrated at radius $r/\sqrt{2}$, then the moment of inertia I about the axis OO will remain the same.

Example 1   The rotating parts of an engine have a mass of 2.4 kg and radius of gyration 100 mm. Determine the torque required to overcome the inertia of the rotating parts when the angular acceleration is 15 rad/s².

$$T = I\alpha = mk^2\alpha$$

where $m = 2.4\,kg$ $k = 100\,mm = 0.1\,m$ and $\alpha = 15\ rad/s^2$

∴ $T = 2.4\,kg \times (0.1\,m)^2 \times 15\ rad/s^2$

   $= 0.36\,Nm$ (since 1 kg m²/s² = 1 Nm)

i.e. the applied torque is 0.36 Nm.

Example 2   An experimental solid-disc flywheel has a mass of 120 kg and an outside diameter of 300 mm. With the flywheel at rest, a constant torque of 10 Nm is applied for a period of 2 seconds. Ignoring the effect of friction, determine for the flywheel (a) the moment of inertia, (b) the angular acceleration, (c) the angular velocity after 2 seconds.

a) $I = mk^2$

where $m = 120\,kg$ and $k^2 = d^2/8 = (0.3\,m)^2/8 = 0.011\,25\ m^2$

∴ $I = 120\,kg \times 0.011\,25\ m^2$

   $= 1.35\ kg\,m^2$

i.e. the moment of inertia is 1.35 kg m².

b) $T = I\alpha$

∴ $\alpha = T/I$

where $T = 10\,Nm$

∴ $\alpha = \dfrac{10\,Nm}{1.35\ kg\,m^2}$

   $= 7.41\ rad/s^2$

i.e. the angular acceleration is 7.41 rad/s².

c)   From section 4.1,

   $\omega_2 = \omega_1 + \alpha t$

where $\omega_1 = 0$ (since the flywheel is initially at rest)   and $t = 2\,s$

∴ $\omega_2 = 0 + (7.41\ rad/s^2 \times 2\,s)$

   $= 14.82\ rad/s$

i.e. the velocity after 2 seconds is 14.82 rad/s.

Example 3   In an experiment to determine the radius of gyration of an annulus (i.e. a disc with a hole in the centre), the following observations were

93

made: applied torque 6 Nm; angular acceleration 9.2 rad/s²; mass of annulus 14.4 kg. Calculate the radius of gyration.

$$T = I\alpha = mk^2\alpha$$

$$\therefore \quad k = \sqrt{\frac{T}{m\alpha}}$$

where $\quad T = 6\,\text{Nm} \qquad m = 14.4\,\text{kg} \quad$ and $\quad \alpha = 9.2\,\text{rad/s}^2$

$$\therefore \quad k = \sqrt{\frac{6\,\text{Nm}}{14.4\,\text{kg} \times 9.2\,\text{rad/s}^2}}$$

$$= \sqrt{0.0453\,\text{m}^2}$$

$$= 0.213\,\text{m} \quad \text{or} \quad 213\,\text{mm}$$

i.e. the radius of gyration is 213 mm.

4.4 Centripetal acceleration

The disc of radius r shown in fig. 4.5(a) is rotating with uniform angular velocity ω. Relative to the centre of rotation O, the point A has a linear velocity v in a direction perpendicular to OA. This velocity is represented by the vector oa in fig. 4.5(b). In time δt, A will move through distance δs to

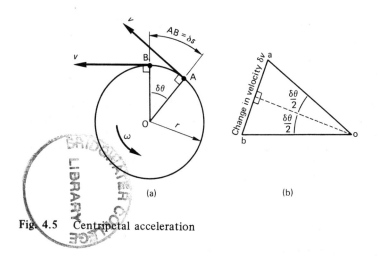

Fig. 4.5 Centripetal acceleration

B. Since the disc is rotating with uniform angular velocity, the linear velocity of B relative to the centre of rotation will also be v. This velocity is represented by the vector ob in fig. 4.5(b). In fig. 4.5(b), the vector ab represents the *change* in velocity δv between A and B,

i.e. change in velocity, $\delta v = ab = 2\,oa\sin\dfrac{\delta\theta}{2}$

But $\delta\theta$ is very small,

$\therefore \quad \sin \dfrac{\delta\theta}{2} \approx \dfrac{\delta\theta}{2}$ radians

$\therefore \quad ab = 2\,oa\,\dfrac{\delta\theta}{2} = oa\,\delta\theta$

or $\quad \delta v = v\delta\theta$

(since $oa = ob = v$)

For there to be a change in velocity there must be an acceleration of magnitude

$$a = \dfrac{\delta v}{\delta t}$$

$$= v\dfrac{\delta\theta}{\delta t}$$

(since the change takes place in time δt)

But $\quad \dfrac{\delta\theta}{\delta t} = \omega$

$\therefore \qquad a = v\omega$

From the relationship between linear and angular motion,

$$v = r\omega$$

$\therefore \quad a = \omega^2 r = \dfrac{v^2}{r}$

The direction of this acceleration is from a towards b in fig. 4.5(b).

Referring to fig. 4.5(b), as $\delta\theta$ approaches zero, the angle oab approaches 90°, thus the direction of the *instantaneous* change in the velocity of A is *towards* the centre of rotation O. For this reason, the acceleration is termed *centripetal acceleration*; i.e. *bodies which move in a circular path have centripetal acceleration, or acceleration towards the centre of rotation, of magnitude*

$$a = \omega^2 r = \dfrac{v^2}{r}$$

which should be remembered.

4.5 Centripetal and centrifugal force

If the point A on the rim of the rotating disc in fig. 4.5(a) has a mass m, then, from Newton's second law of motion, a force of magnitude

$$F = m\omega^2 r = m\dfrac{v^2}{r}$$

95

will act *on* the mass in a direction towards the centre of rotation. This force is known as the *centripetal force*,

i.e.   centripetal force $= m\omega^2 r = m\dfrac{v^2}{r}$

From Newton's third law of motion, if a force acts *on* the mass, the mass will exert a reaction force on its surroundings which is equal in magnitude but opposite in direction to the applied force. If the applied force causes the mass to accelerate, the reaction force is known as the *inertia force*. For the special case of a mass moving in a circular path, the reaction or inertia force is called the *centrifugal force*; i.e. the centrifugal force has the same magnitude as the centripetal force but its direction is *outwards* from the centre of rotation. Thus

centrifugal force $= m\omega^2 r = m\dfrac{v^2}{r}$

Typical examples of centripetal and centrifugal forces are

a) the hammer thrower in fig. 4.6 is exerting a *centripetal* force on the hammer head by *pulling* on the wire, while he *feels* a *centrifugal* force pulling outwards on his hands;

Fig. 4.6   Hammer thrower

b) the 'wall-of-death' motor-cyclist at the fun-fair is prevented from moving outwards because the wall exerts a *centripetal* force on the machine; the machine is applying a *centrifugal* force to the wall;
c) as a train rounds a curve, the outer rail exerts a *centripetal* force on the train while the train exerts a *centrifugal* force on the rail.

Thus centripetal forces act *inwards on the mass* and centrifugal forces act *outwards on the surroundings*. Both forces are of magnitude

$F = m\omega^2 r = m\dfrac{v^2}{r}$

which should be remembered.

Example 1 A casting on a lathe faceplate has a mass of 20 kg which can be considered to be concentrated at a radius of 220 mm. Determine the radial force acting on the spindle bearings when the faceplate is rotating at 90 rev/min. What is the name of this radial force?

Since the casting on the faceplate is rotating, it will exert a *centrifugal* force on the spindle bearings; i.e. the name of the radial force acting on the spindle bearings is *centrifugal force*. Note that the bearings are exerting a *centripetal* force *on* the casting.

Centrifugal force $F = m\omega^2 r$

where $m = 20\,\text{kg}$ $\omega = \dfrac{90 \text{ rev/min} \times 2\pi \text{ rad/rev}}{60 \text{ s/min}} = 9.42 \text{ rad/s}$

and $r = 220\,\text{mm} = 0.22\,\text{m}$

∴ $F = 20\,\text{kg} \times (9.42 \text{ rad/s})^2 \times 0.22\,\text{m}$

          $= 390.4\,\text{N}$

i.e. the radial or centrifugal force on the spindle is 390.4 N.

Example 2 The vehicle shown in fig. 4.7 is travelling at constant speed v round a level curve of mean radius r. The centre of gravity G of the vehicle is at height h above the road surface, the wheel-track width is $2d$, and the coefficient of friction between the tyres and the road surface is μ. If the mass of the vehicle is m, derive expressions for the maximum speed at which the vehicle can negotiate the curve if it is not to (a) skid, (b) overturn. Compare the equations and state the limiting conditions.

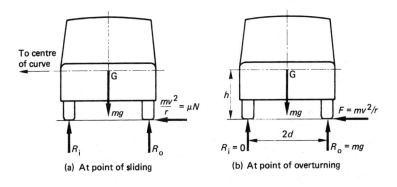

(a) At point of sliding   (b) At point of overturning

Fig. 4.7

a) Referring to fig. 4.7(a), let the normal reaction at the inner wheel be R_i and the normal reaction at the outer wheel be R_o. As the vehicle rounds the

97

curve, the frictional force between the tyres and the road surface exerts a *centripetal* force on the vehicle. Thus

$$\text{maximum centripetal force} = \text{limiting frictional force}$$

i.e.

$$m\frac{v^2}{r} = \mu R_i + \mu R_o$$

but $\quad R_i + R_o = mg$

$$\therefore \quad m\frac{v^2}{r} = \mu mg$$

or $\quad v = \sqrt{\mu rg}$

which should be remembered.

Notice that the velocity v is independent of the mass m.

b) Referring to fig. 4.7(b), the vehicle will be on the point of overturning when the reaction at the inner wheel R_i is zero. Letting $R_i = 0$, take moments about the centre of gravity G:

$$\Sigma \text{ clockwise moments} = \Sigma \text{ anticlockwise moments}$$

$\therefore \qquad\qquad\qquad\qquad Fh = R_o d$

i.e.

$$m\frac{v^2}{r}h = mgd$$

or

$$v = \sqrt{\frac{d}{h}rg}$$

which should be remembered.

Comparing the equations, the vehicle will *skid* when μ is *less* than d/h and will *overturn* when μ is *greater* than d/h, *which should be remembered.*

Example 3   A vehicle has a wheel-track width of 1.8 m and its centre of gravity is 1.2 m above the road surface. Find the maximum safe speed at which the vehicle can travel round a level curve of mean radius 40 m. The coefficient of friction between the tyres and the road surface is 0.55.

The maximum safe speed will be determined by the values of the ratio d/h and the coefficient of friction μ.

Now $\quad d = (1.8\,\text{m})/2 = 0.9\,\text{m} \quad$ and $\quad h = 1.2\,\text{m}$

$$\therefore \quad \frac{d}{h} = \frac{0.9\,\text{m}}{1.2\,\text{m}} = 0.75$$

which is greater than the value for μ (0.55); therefore the vehicle will skid and the maximum safe speed is

$$v = \sqrt{\mu rg}$$

where $r = 40\,\text{m}$ and $g = 9.81\,\text{m/s}^2$

$\therefore \quad v = \sqrt{(0.55 \times 40\,\text{m} \times 9.81\,\text{m/s}^2)}$

$\qquad = 14.69\,\text{m/s}$ or $52.9\,\text{km/h}$

i.e. the maximum safe speed is $52.9\,\text{km/h}$.

Example 4   The centre of gravity of a motor cycle and its rider is $0.7\,\text{m}$ above the road surface with the machine in an upright position. If the coefficient of friction between the tyres and the road surface is 0.6, calculate (a) the maximum speed at which the combination can safely negotiate a level curve of mean radius $50\,\text{m}$ without sideways slip, (b) the magnitude of the necessary heel-over angle measured from the vertical.

a) For no sideways slip,

$$v = \sqrt{\mu r g}$$

where $\mu = 0.6$ $\quad r = 50\,\text{m}$ and $g = 9.81\,\text{m/s}^2$

$\therefore \quad v = \sqrt{(0.6 \times 50\,\text{m} \times 9.81\,\text{m/s}^2)}$

$\qquad = 17.16\,\text{m/s}$ or $61.8\,\text{km/h}$

i.e. the maximum speed is $61.8\,\text{km/h}$.

b) As the motor-cyclist rounds the curve, he leans in towards the centre to balance the combined effect of the centripetal force and the normal reaction at the road surface, as shown in fig. 4.8. Referring to fig. 4.8, take moments about the centre of gravity G:

Fig. 4.8

$$\Sigma \text{ clockwise moments } = \Sigma \text{ anticlockwise moments}$$

$$\therefore \qquad mg \times 0.7 \sin\theta = F \times 0.7 \cos\theta$$

or
$$\frac{\sin\theta}{\cos\theta} = \frac{F}{mg}$$

But $\dfrac{\sin\theta}{\cos\theta} = \tan\theta$ and $F = m\dfrac{v^2}{r}$

$$\therefore \quad \tan\theta = \frac{mv^2/r}{mg} = \frac{v^2}{rg}$$

where $v = 17.16\,\text{m/s}$ $\quad r = 50\,\text{m}$ and $g = 9.81\,\text{m/s}^2$

$$\therefore \quad \tan\theta = \frac{(17.16\,\text{m/s}^2)}{50\,\text{m} \times 9.81\,\text{m/s}^2} = 0.5996$$

$$\therefore \qquad \theta = 30.9°$$

i.e. the heel-over angle is 30.9° measured from the vertical.

Alternatively, for the motor cycle and rider to negotiate the bend safely, the *line of action of the resultant* of the normal reaction at the road surface and the centripetal force must pass through the centre of gravity G, *which it is useful to remember.*

$$\therefore \quad \tan\theta = \frac{mv^2/r}{mg}$$

which will yield $\theta = 30.9°$ as before.

This latter concept can be applied to vehicles travelling round curved tracks, as illustrated in the following example.

Example 5 The vehicle shown in fig. 4.9 is travelling at constant speed v round a banked curve inclined at angle θ, measured from the horizontal, and

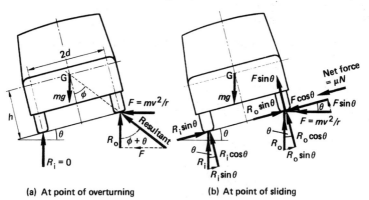

(a) At point of overturning (b) At point of sliding

Fig. 4.9

having a mean radius r. The centre of gravity G is at height h above the road surface, the wheel-track width is $2d$, and the coefficient of friction between the tyres and the road surface is μ. If the mass of the vehicle is m, derive expressions for the maximum speed at which the vehicle can negotiate the curve if it is not to (a) overturn, (b) skid. Compare the equations and state the limiting conditions.

a) At the point of overturning, the reaction at the inner wheel $R_i = 0$, and at the outer wheel $R_o = mg$. The resultant of the reaction R_o and the centripetal force F will also pass through the centre of gravity G, as shown in fig. 4.9(a).

Referring to fig. 4.9(a),

$$\tan(\phi + \theta) = \frac{F}{R_o}$$

But $F = mv^2/r \qquad R_o = mg$

and $\tan(\phi + \theta) = \dfrac{\tan\phi + \tan\theta}{1 - \tan\phi \tan\theta} = \dfrac{d/h + \tan\theta}{1 - (d/h)\tan\theta}$

since $d/h = \tan\phi$

$$\therefore \quad \frac{mv^2/r}{mg} = \frac{d/h + \tan\theta}{1 - (d/h)\tan\theta}$$

or $\qquad v = \sqrt{rg\dfrac{d/h + \tan\theta}{1 - (d/h)\tan\theta}}$

which should be remembered.

b) At the point of sliding, the sum of the components of the reactions R_i R_o and the centripetal force F parallel to the road surface will equal the friction force μN. The normal reaction N is the sum of the components of the reactions at R_i and R_o and the centripetal force F normal to the road surface, as shown in fig. 4.9(b).

Referring to fig. 4.9(b),

$$F\cos\theta - R_i\sin\theta - R_o\sin\theta = \mu(R_i\cos\theta + R_o\cos\theta + F\sin\theta)$$

But $R_i + R_o = mg$ and $F = mv^2/r$

and dividing both sides by $\cos\theta$ gives

$$mv^2/r - mg\tan\theta = \mu[mg^2 + (mv^2/r)\tan\theta]$$

$$\therefore \quad \frac{v^2}{r}(1 - \mu\tan\theta) = g(\mu + \tan\theta)$$

or $\qquad v = \sqrt{rg\dfrac{\mu + \tan\theta}{1 - \mu\tan\theta}}$

which should be remembered.

Comparing the equations, the vehicle will *skid* when μ is *less* than d/h and will *overturn* when μ is *greater* than d/h, *which should be remembered.*

Example 6 The centre of gravity of a vehicle is 2 m above the road surface and its wheel-track width is 2.1 m. Find the maximum safe speed the vehicle can travel round a 15° banked curve (measured from the horizontal) at a mean radius of 45 m. The coefficient of friction is 0.65.

The maximum safe speed will be determined by the values of the ratio d/h and the coefficient of friction μ.

Now $d = (2.1\,\text{m})/2 = 1.05\,\text{m}$ and $h = 2\,\text{m}$

$\therefore \quad \dfrac{d}{h} = \dfrac{1.05\,\text{m}}{2\,\text{m}} = 0.525$

which is *less* than the value for μ (0.65); therefore the vehicle will overturn and the maximum safe speed is

$$v = \sqrt{rg\,\frac{d/h + \tan\theta}{1 - (d/h)\tan\theta}}$$

where $r = 45\,\text{m}$ $g = 9.81\,\text{m/s}^2$ and $\theta = 15°$

$\therefore \quad v = \sqrt{45\,\text{m} \times 9.81\,\text{m/s}^2 \left(\dfrac{0.525 + \tan 15°}{1 - 0.525 \tan 15°} \right)}$

$\qquad = 20.18\,\text{m/s}$ or $72.7\,\text{km/h}$

i.e. the maximum speed is 72.7 km/h.

Example 7 A casting attached to a lathe faceplate may be considered as two masses of magnitude 4 kg and 3 kg acting at radii 200 mm and 180 mm respectively, the angular relationship between them being as shown in fig. 4.10(a). With the faceplate rotating at 180 rev/min, calculate (a) the centripetal force exerted on the spindle bearing, (b) the magnitude and angular position of the mass acting at a radius of 200 mm required to statically balance the faceplate and thus eliminate the centripetal force acting on the spindle bearing.

a) Centripetal force $F = m\,\omega^2 r$

At position A, $m = 4\,\text{kg}$ $r = 0.2\,\text{m}$ and

$\qquad\qquad \omega = \dfrac{180\,\text{rev/min}}{60\,\text{s/min}} \times 2\pi\,\text{rad/rev} = 18.85\,\text{rad/s}$

$\therefore \quad F_A = 4\,\text{kg} \times (18.85\,\text{rad/s})^2 \times 0.2\,\text{m}$

$\qquad = 284.2\,\text{N}$

102

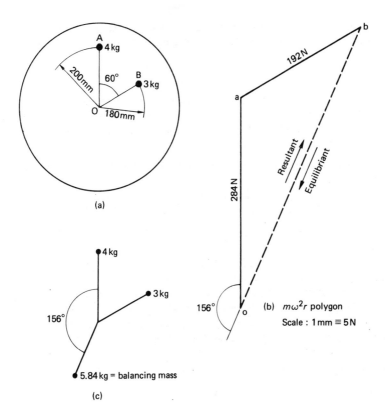

Fig. 4.10

At position B, $m = 3\,\text{kg}$ and $r = 0.18\,\text{m}$

∴ $F_B = 3\,\text{kg} \times (18.85\,\text{rad/s})^2 \times 0.18\,\text{m}$

$= 192\,\text{N}$

To find the resultant force on the spindle bearing, these forces must be added vectorially as shown in fig. 4.10(b). Referring to fig. 4.10(b), where $1\,\text{mm} \equiv 5\,\text{N}$,

i) draw vector *oa* 56.8 mm long and parallel to the radius arm OA in fig. 4.10(a);
ii) draw vector *ab* 38.4 mm long and parallel to the radius arm OB;
iii) join ob.

The vector *ob* represents the *resultant* force on the spindle in magnitude and direction, i.e. o *towards* b, and scales 83.0 mm,

∴ resultant force = 83.0 mm × 5 N/mm

$= 415\,\text{N}$

i.e. the resultant force on the spindle is 415 N.

b) In fig. 4.10(b), the vector **bo** represents the *equilibriant* in magnitude and direction, i.e. b *towards* o, and is of magnitude 415 N.

Balancing mass $m = F/\omega^2 r$

where $\omega = 18.85\,\text{rad/s}$ and $r = 0.2\,\text{m}$

$$\therefore\ m = \frac{415\,\text{N}}{(18.85\,\text{rad/s})^2 \times 0.2\,\text{m}}$$

$$= 5.84\,\text{kg}$$

i.e. the balancing mass required is 5.84 kg and its angular position is as shown in fig. 4.10(c).

Notice that in this example the balancing mass was found from the closing vector in the $m\omega^2 r$ polygon. Since the term ω^2 is common to each vector, it is only necessary to consider the mass–radius (mr) product for each mass to find the magnitude and angular position of the balancing mass. This is illustrated in the following example.

Example 8 On a rotating disc, three masses of magnitude 0.2 kg, 0.1 kg, and 0.15 kg are located at radii 40 mm, 45 mm, and 30 mm respectively. The angular relationship between the masses is shown in fig. 4.11(a). Find the angular position and magnitude of the mass required at a radius of 50 mm to statically balance the disc.

Referring to fig. 4.11(a), at A

$$m_A r_A = 0.2\,\text{kg} \times 40\,\text{mm} = 8\,\text{kg mm}$$

at B

$$m_B r_B = 0.1\,\text{kg} \times 45\,\text{mm} = 4.5\,\text{kg mm}$$

and at C

$$m_C r_C = 0.15\,\text{kg} \times 30\,\text{mm} = 4.5\,\text{kg mm}$$

Using these values, the mr polygon shown in fig. 4.11(b) has been drawn. Referring to fig. 4.11(b), where $1\,\text{mm} \equiv 0.2\,\text{kg mm}$, vector **oa** is 40 mm long and has been drawn parallel to the radius arm OA in fig. 4.11(a), vector **ab** is 22.5 mm long and is parallel to OB, and vector **bc** is 22.5 mm long and is parallel to OC. The closing vector, **co**, is 39.5 mm long and represents the balancing product $m_D r_D$.

$$\therefore\ m_D r_D = 39.5\,\text{mm} \times 0.2\,\text{kg mm/mm}$$

$$= 7.9\,\text{kg mm}$$

but $r_D = 50\,\text{mm}$

$$\therefore\ m_D = \frac{7.9\,\text{kg mm}}{50\,\text{mm}}$$

$$= 0.158\,\text{kg}$$

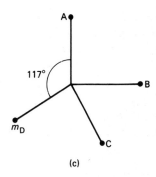

Fig. 4.11

i.e. the balancing mass is 0.158 kg and its angular position is as shown in fig. 4.11(c).

Exercises on chapter 4

1 The speed of a flywheel is increased uniformly from 210 rev/min to 250 rev/min in 5 seconds. Determine the angular acceleration and the number of revolutions made by the wheel in the 5-second period.
[0.84 rad/s²; 19.2 revs]

2 A grinding wheel is rotating at 2800 rev/min when the power is switched off. If it takes 4 minutes for the wheel to come to rest, calculate the angular retardation, assuming it to be uniform. [1.22 rad/s²]

3 A lift winding drum accelerates uniformly from rest for 1.5 seconds until it is rotating at 80 rev/min. At this speed, the drum makes 2.6 revolutions before coming uniformly to rest in 1.2 seconds. Determine (a) the angular acceleration and retardation, (b) the total time the drum is rotating, (c) the

total number of revolutions made by the drum.
[5.6 rad/s^2; 7 rad/s^2; 4.65 s; 4.4 revs]

4 The flywheel of an internal-combustion engine is accelerated uniformly at 15 rad/s^2 for 3 seconds, until the engine speed is 3500 rev/min. What is the initial speed? If the rotating parts of the engine have a moment of inertia of 1.3 kg m^2, determine the accelerating torque. [3070 rev/min; 19.5 Nm]

5 Define 'radius of gyration'.

The mass of a flywheel can be assumed to be concentrated at a radius of 215 mm. If the torque required to give the flywheel an angular acceleration of 6 rad/s^2 is 11 Nm, estimate the mass of the flywheel. [39.7 kg]

6 An experimental solid-disc flywheel is 300 mm diameter and has a mass of 70 kg. Experiments show that, at all speeds of rotation, the frictional resistance to motion is equivalent to a torque of 0.15 Nm. If when the flywheel is rotating at 50 rev/min the driving power is removed, calculate (a) the angular retardation, (b) the time taken for the flywheel to come to rest, (c) the total number of revolutions made by the flywheel during retardation. [0.19 rad/s^2; 27.6 s; 11.5 revs]

7 A car wheel and tyre, having a mass of 35 kg and a rolling diameter of 0.61 m, is balanced with the wheel rotating at an equivalent road speed of 112 km/h. If a torque of 20 Nm is required to accelerate the wheel uniformly to its running speed in 5 seconds, calculate the radius of gyration of the wheel and tyre. [0.167 m]

8 A mass of 60 g is required to balance a motor-car wheel. If the mass is attached to the 0.33 m diameter rim, calculate the centrifugal force acting on the rim when the wheel is rotating at 470 rev/min. [24 N]

9 The pick-up arm on a record player has an effective mass of 2.5 g at all positions on the turntable. What is the centrifugal force acting on a record playing at $33\frac{1}{3}$ rev/min when the stylus is at a radius of 145 mm? Will the force increase or decrease as the stylus moves towards the centre of the record? [0.0044 N; decrease]

10 When negotiating a curve on a level road, a cyclist is limited to a heel-over angle of 15° measured from the vertical. Determine the maximum speed at which the cyclist can safely round a curve of 40 m radius. [36.9 km/h]

11 The coefficient of friction between the tyres of a motor cycle and the vertical wall of the 'wall of death' at the fun-fair is 0.6. Calculate the minimum speed the rider must attain before moving on to the vertical wall where the diameter is 20 m. If the combined mass of rider and machine is 370 kg, what is the centrifugal force acting on the wall? [46 km/h; 6.05 kN]

12 A vehicle with a track width of 1.6 m and centre of gravity 1.4 m above the road surface rounds a level curve of mean radius 60 m. If the coefficient of friction between the tyres and the road surface is 0.65, determine the limiting speed. [66 km/h]

13 If the vehicle in question 12 rounds a 10° banked curve of mean radius 50 m, determine the limiting speed. [72.7 km/h]

14 If the stall speed of an aircraft is 150 km/h, what is the minimum diameter at which it can 'loop the loop' (i.e. turn in a circle whose axis is parallel with the ground)? When turning in this circle, determine the force acting on the aircraft when it is at the bottom of the loop, if the mass of the aircraft is 1200 kg.   [354 m; 23.54 kN]

15   A disc has a mass of 1.4 tonne (1 tonne = 1000 kg) and is accelerated from rest at the rate of 2 rad/s². If the diameter of the disc is 1.5 m, calculate (a) the radius of gyration of the disc, (b) the accelerating torque, (c) the speed of the disc, in rev/min, after 10 seconds, (d) the total number of revolutions made by the disc in 10 seconds.
[0.53 m; 787.5 N m; 191 rev/min; 15.9 rev]

16   A point on the periphery of a rotating disc has an instantaneous linear velocity of 42 m/s. If the diameter of the disc is 350 mm, calculate (a) the angular velocity of the disc, (b) the angular acceleration of the disc if, after 20 seconds, the instantaneous linear velocity of the same point has increased uniformly to 85 m/s.   [240 rad/s; 12.29 rad/s²]

17   A vehicle having a mass of 4 tonne is travelling round a level curve of mean radius 20 m at a speed of 20 km/h. The track width is 2 m and the surface of the vehicle can be taken as equivalent to a rectangle 4.5 m high and 6.5 m long with the centre of area 2.25 m above the road surface. If the centre of gravity is 1.5 m above the road surface, find the least wind pressure which would overturn the vehicle.   [455.6 N/m²]

18   Three masses − 4 kg, 2 kg, and 6 kg − rotate in the same plane at radii 125 mm, 75 mm, and 100 mm respectively. The 2 kg and 6 kg masses are at angular displacements 80° and 170° respectively, both measured anticlockwise from the 4 kg mass. Find (a) the magnitude of the out-of-balance force when the masses rotate at 150 rev/min, (b) the magnitude and angular position relative to the 4 kg mass of the mass required at a radius of 200 mm for the system to be perfectly balanced.   [64.2N; 1.3 kg at 75.6°]

19   The mass of a casting which is attached to the faceplate of a lathe may be assumed to be concentrated at two points A and B. At A, the mass is 15 kg and the radius from the spindle centre is 250 mm. At B, which is 135° clockwise from A, the mass is 27 kg and the radius is 200 mm. Find the magnitude and angular position, relative to the larger mass, of the mass which must be placed at a radius of 250 mm to reduce the centripetal force on the spindle bearing to zero.   [15.28 kg at 136°]

5 Kinetic energy

5.1 Introduction
A body which is in motion possesses *kinetic energy*. The amount of kinetic energy in the body depends upon the *mass* and the *velocity* of the body.

There are two forms of kinetic energy:

i) *translatory* or *linear*;
ii) *rotational* or *angular*.

5.2 Translatory or linear kinetic energy
Consider the stationary body of mass m shown in fig. 5.1(a) at position A. When acted upon by the force F, the body moves with uniform acceleration a to position B in time t. At B, the body has a velocity v. The motion of the body is illustrated in the velocity-time graph, fig. 5.1(b).

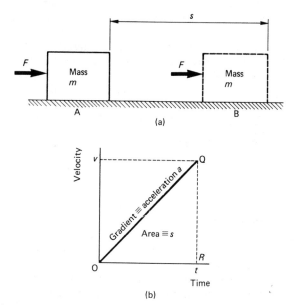

Fig. 5.1   Translatory or linear kinetic energy

Work done on the body = force x distance moved by the body

i.e. $$W = Fs$$

From Newton's second law of motion,

force F = mass × acceleration

i.e. $F = ma$

$\therefore$ $W = mas$

From the velocity–time graph, fig. 5.1(b),

acceleration $a \equiv$ gradient or slope of the line OQ $= \dfrac{v}{t}$

and distance travelled $s \equiv$ area OQR $= \frac{1}{2}vt$

$\therefore$ $W = m\dfrac{v}{t} \cdot \frac{1}{2}vt$

$\qquad = \frac{1}{2}mv^2$

At position B, the body possesses kinetic energy, the amount being equal to the work done on the body,

i.e. kinetic energy (k.e.) = work W done on the body

or $\qquad\qquad$ k.e. $= \frac{1}{2}mv^2$

which should be remembered.

The unit for kinetic energy is the *joule* (J).

Example A milling-machine table, milling fixture, and component have a combined mass of 370 kg. Determine the kinetic energy when the table is being rapidly traversed at 40 mm/s.

$\qquad$ k.e. $= \frac{1}{2}mv^2$

where m = 370 kg and v = 40 mm/s = 0.04 m/s

$\therefore$ k.e. $= \frac{1}{2} \times 370$ kg $\times (0.04$ m/s$)^2$

$\qquad\quad = 0.296$ J

i.e. the kinetic energy is 0.296 J.

5.3 Rotational or angular kinetic energy

The elemental mass δm at radius r in fig. 5.2 is rotating about O with an angular velocity ω. At the instant shown, the elemental mass also has a *tangential* or *linear* velocity v.

The *linear* kinetic energy possessed by δm is given by $\frac{1}{2}\delta mv^2$.

From the relationship between linear and angular motion,

$\qquad v = r\omega$

$\therefore$ kinetic energy $= \frac{1}{2}\delta m\,(r\omega)^2$

and total kinetic energy $= \Sigma\frac{1}{2}\delta mr^2\omega^2$

109

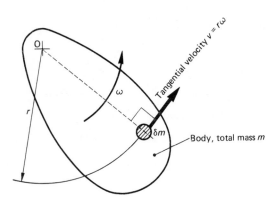

Fig. 5.2   Rotational or angular kinetic energy

From section 4.2,

$$\Sigma \, \delta m r^2 = I \quad \text{(the moment of inertia of the body about O)}$$

and $\qquad I = mk^2$

where $\quad k$ = radius of gyration about O

$\therefore$ total *angular* kinetic energy (k.e.) $= \frac{1}{2}I\omega^2 = \frac{1}{2}mk^2\omega^2$

which should be remembered.

The unit for angular kinetic energy is the *joule* (J).

Example   A winding drum has a mass of 950 kg and radius of gyration 0.82 m. Determine the kinetic energy in the drum when it is rotating at 45 rev/min.

$$\text{k.e.} = \frac{1}{2}I\omega^2 = \frac{1}{2}mk^2\omega^2$$

where $\quad m$ = 950 kg $\qquad k$ = 0.82 m

and $\qquad \omega = \dfrac{45 \text{ rev/min} \times 2\pi \text{ rad/rev}}{60 \text{ s/min}} = 4.71 \text{ rad/s}$

$\therefore$ k.e. $= \frac{1}{2} \times 950 \text{ kg} \times (0.82 \text{ m})^2 \times (4.71 \text{ rad/s})^2$

$\qquad \quad = 7085 \text{ J}$

i.e. the kinetic energy in the drum is 7085 J.

5.4 Total kinetic energy of a body having both linear and angular motion
The body shown in fig. 5.3(a) is rotating about its centre of gravity G with an angular velocity ω, and at the same time has a linear velocity v. (An example of this condition is a rolling wheel.) At the instant shown, the elemental mass

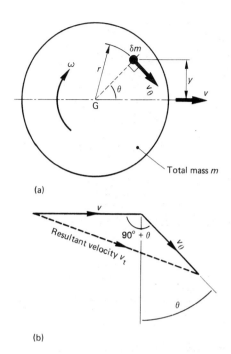

(a)

(b)

Fig. 5.3 Total kinetic energy

δm at radius r has a *tangential* or *linear* velocity v_θ. The *resultant* or *total* velocity v_t of the elemental mass with respect to the centre of gravity G may be found by vectorial addition as shown in fig. 5.3(b).

From fig. 5.3(b) and using the cosine rule,

$$v_t^2 = v^2 + v_\theta^2 - 2vv_\theta \cos(90° + \theta)$$

But $\cos(90° + \theta) = \sin\theta = y/r$

and, from the relationship between linear and angular motion,

$$v_\theta = r\omega$$

$$\therefore \quad v_t^2 = v^2 + (r\omega)^2 - 2v(r\omega)\frac{y}{r}$$

$$= v^2 + r^2\omega^2 - 2yv\omega$$

The kinetic energy possessed by δm is given by $\frac{1}{2}\delta m v_t^2$

and total kinetic energy $= \Sigma \frac{1}{2}\delta m v_t^2$

$$= \Sigma \frac{1}{2}\delta m \left(v^2 + r^2\omega^2 - 2yv\omega\right)$$

$$= \Sigma \frac{1}{2}\delta m v^2 + \Sigma \frac{1}{2}\delta m r^2 \omega^2 - \Sigma \delta m y v\omega$$

111

The term δmy is the first moment of the elemental mass about the centre of gravity and, by definition, $\Sigma \delta my$ about the centre of gravity is zero,

i.e. $\quad \Sigma \delta my = 0$

$\therefore \quad$ total kinetic energy $= \frac{1}{2} mv^2 + \frac{1}{2} I \omega^2$

i.e. when a body has both linear and angular velocity, the total kinetic energy is the sum of the linear and angular kinetic energies, *which should be remembered.*

Example 1 A solid disc, having an outside diameter of 0.5 m and a mass of 151 kg, rolls without slipping along a level surface with a velocity of 2 m/s. What is the total kinetic energy in the disc?

$$\text{Total k.e.} = \frac{1}{2} mv^2 + \frac{1}{2} I \omega^2$$
$$= \frac{1}{2} m (v^2 + k^2 \omega^2)$$

since $\quad I = mk^2$

where $\quad m = 151 \text{ kg} \qquad v = 2 \text{ m/s} \qquad \omega = \frac{v}{r} = \frac{2 \text{ m/s}}{0.25 \text{ m}} = 8 \text{ rad/s}$

and, for a solid disc, $\quad k^2 = d^2/8 = (0.5 \text{ m})^2/8 = 0.031\,25 \text{ m}^2$

$\therefore \quad$ total k.e. $= \frac{1}{2} \times 151 \text{ kg} \times [(2 \text{ m/s})^2 + 0.031\,25 \text{ m}^2 \times (8 \text{ rad/s})^2]$

$\qquad\qquad = 453 \text{ J}$

i.e. the total kinetic energy in the disc is 453 J.

Example 2 The outside diameter and moment of inertia of a lift winding drum are 1.6 m and 130 kg m² respectively. The lift cage has a mass of 300 kg. Ignoring the effect of the rope, calculate the total kinetic energy in the system when the cage is being raised at a uniform speed of 1.2 m/s.

$$\text{Total k.e.} = \frac{1}{2} mv^2 + \frac{1}{2} I \omega^2$$

where $\quad m = 300 \text{ kg} \qquad v = 1.2 \text{ m/s} \qquad I = 130 \text{ kg m}^2$

and $\quad \omega = \frac{v}{r} = \frac{1.2 \text{ m/s}}{0.8 \text{ m}} = 1.5 \text{ rad/s}$

$\therefore \quad$ total k.e. $= [\frac{1}{2} \times 300 \text{ kg} \times (1.2 \text{ m/s})^2] + [\frac{1}{2} \times 130 \text{ kg m}^2 \times (1.5 \text{ rad/s})^2]$

$\qquad\qquad = 216 \text{ J} + 146.25 \text{ J}$

$\qquad\qquad = 362.25 \text{ J}$

i.e. the total kinetic energy in the system is 362.25 J.

Example 3 The motor in a power press rotates at five times the speed of the driven flywheel. The flywheel is required to provide 40 kJ of energy while its speed is reduced from 210 rev/min to 150 rev/min. Determine the moment of inertia of the flywheel. If the speed of the flywheel is increased uniformly from 150 rev/min to 210 rev/min in 15 seconds and the efficiency of the drive is 75%, determine the torque at the motor shaft.

Change in kinetic energy $= \frac{1}{2}I(\omega_2^2 - \omega_1^2)$

$\therefore$ $$I = \frac{2 \times \text{change in k.e.}}{\omega_2^2 - \omega_1^2}$$

where change in k.e. $= 40\,\text{kJ} = 40 \times 10^3\,\text{J}$

$$\omega_1 = \frac{150\ \text{rev/min} \times 2\pi\ \text{rad/rev}}{60\ \text{s/min}} = 15.7\ \text{rad/s}$$

and $$\omega_2 = \frac{210\ \text{rev/min} \times 2\pi\ \text{rad/rev}}{60\ \text{s/min}} = 22\ \text{rad/s}$$

$\therefore$ $$I = \frac{2 \times 40 \times 10^3\,\text{J}}{(22\ \text{rad/s})^2 - (15.7\ \text{rad/s})^2}$$

$$= 336.8\ \text{kgm}^2$$

i.e. the moment of inertia is $336.8\ \text{kgm}^2$.

From section 4.1,

angular acceleration $\alpha = (\omega_2 - \omega_1)/t$

where $t = 15\ \text{s}$

$\therefore$ $$\alpha = \frac{22\ \text{rad/s} - 15.7\ \text{rad/s}}{15\ \text{s}}$$

$$= 0.42\ \text{rad/s}^2$$

From section 4.2,

torque at the flywheel $T_f = I\alpha$

$$= 336.8\ \text{kgm}^2 \times 0.42\ \text{rad/s}^2$$

$$= 141.5\ \text{Nm}$$

The efficiency of the drive, η (*eta*), is given by

$$\eta = \frac{\text{power output}}{\text{power input}}$$

i.e. $$\eta = \frac{T_f \omega_f}{T_m \omega_m}$$

$\therefore$ torque at motor shaft $T_m = \dfrac{T_f \omega_f}{\eta \omega_m}$

where ω_f = speed of flywheel ω_m = motor speed $= 5\,\omega_f$

and $\eta = 75\% = 0.75$

$$\therefore \quad T_m = \frac{141.5 \, \text{Nm} \times \omega_f}{0.75 \times 5 \, \omega_f}$$

$$= 37.7 \, \text{Nm}$$

i.e. the torque at the motor shaft is 37.7 Nm.

Example 4 An electric motor, which provides a constant output power of 5 kW when rotating at 1440 rev/min, drives a flywheel through a 4:1 reduction gearbox and slipping clutch, the drive being 80% efficient. If it takes 5 seconds for the flywheel to attain its normal running speed, determine its moment of inertia. What will be the kinetic energy in the flywheel at the normal running speed?

$$P = T\omega$$

$$\therefore \quad T = P/\omega$$

where $\quad P = 5 \, \text{kW} = 5 \times 10^3 \, \text{W}$

and $\quad \omega_m = \dfrac{1440 \, \text{rev/min} \times 2\pi \, \text{rad/rev}}{60 \, \text{s/min}} = 150.8 \, \text{rad/s}$

$$\therefore \quad T_m = \frac{5 \times 10^3 \, \text{W}}{150.8 \, \text{rad/s}}$$

$$= 33.16 \, \text{Nm}$$

$$= \text{torque at the motor shaft}$$

$$\eta = \frac{\text{power output}}{\text{power input}} = \frac{T_f \omega_f}{T_m \omega_m}$$

$\therefore$ torque at the flywheel $T_f = \eta T_m \dfrac{\omega_m}{\omega_f}$

where $\quad \eta = 0.8 \quad$ and $\quad \omega_f = \omega_m/4 = 37.7 \, \text{rad/s}$

$$\therefore \quad T_f = 0.8 \times 33.16 \, \text{Nm} \times \frac{150.8 \, \text{rad/s}}{37.7 \, \text{rad/s}}$$

$$= 106.11 \, \text{Nm}$$

$$T_f = I\alpha$$

$$\therefore \quad I = T_f/\alpha$$

and $\quad \alpha = \dfrac{\omega_2 - \omega_1}{t} = \dfrac{37.7 \, \text{rad/s} - 0}{5 \, \text{s}} = 7.54 \, \text{rad/s}^2$

$$\therefore \quad I = \frac{106.11 \, \text{Nm}}{7.54 \, \text{rad/s}}$$

$$= 14.07 \, \text{kgm}^2$$

i.e. the moment of inertia is 14.07 kgm².

$$\text{Angular kinetic energy} = \tfrac{1}{2}I\omega_f^2$$

$$= \tfrac{1}{2} \times 14.07 \text{ kg m}^2 \times (37.7 \text{ rad/s})^2$$

$$= 10\,000 \text{ J} \quad \text{or} \quad 10 \text{ kJ}$$

i.e. the kinetic energy is 10 kJ.

Exercises on chapter 5

1 Calculate the translatory kinetic energy in a vehicle of mass 900 kg travelling with a speed of 60 km/h.   [125 kJ]

2 A flywheel of mass 150 kg has a radius of gyration of 450 mm and is rotating at 300 rev/min. Calculate the kinetic energy in the flywheel. [15 kJ]

3 The rotating parts of an engine may be considered to have a mass of 3.5 kg acting at a radius of gyration of 0.1 m. If the mass of the engine itself is 80 kg, determine the total kinetic energy in the engine when it is propelling the vehicle at 40 km/h while rotating at 2100 rev/min.   [5.78 kJ]

4 A solid disc of mass 15 kg and outside diameter 150 mm is allowed to roll from rest down a plane which is inclined at 6° to the horizontal. If there is no slipping between the disc and the surface, determine the total kinetic energy in the disc when it has travelled 3 m down the incline. What will be its linear velocity and speed of rotation (in rev/min) at this point? (Hint: at the top of the incline, the disc will possess only potential energy.) [46.14 J; 2.027 m/s; 258 rev/min]

5 A lift winding drum is 600 mm diameter and has a moment of inertia of 115 kg m², while the lift cage has a mass of 700 kg. Ignoring the effect of the rope, determine the total kinetic energy in the lift system when the drum is rotating at 60 rev/min.   [3513.6 J]

6 The motor driving the winding drum in question 5 rotates at 1410 rev/min. If the efficiency of the drive between the drum and the motor shaft is 65%, determine the torque at the motor to accelerate the lift system from rest to its running speed of 60 rev/min in 3 seconds.   [159.27 N m]

7 A flywheel of mass 8 tonne (1 tonne = 1000 kg) has a radius of gyration of 1.6 m. Determine the kinetic energy in the flywheel when it is rotating at 90 rev/min. If the speed of the flywheel is reduced to 80 rev/min, what will be the change in kinetic energy.   [909.6 kJ; 190.9 kJ]

8 A press flywheel with a radius of gyration of 0.5 m and a mass of 900 kg is rotating at 480 rev/min. Determine the kinetic energy in the flywheel. If 10% of this energy is required during a press operation, determine the percentage reduction in the speed of the flywheel.   [284 kJ; 5.13%]

9 A flywheel stores 500 kJ of kinetic energy when rotating at 250 rev/min. What will be the speed when the kinetic energy is reduced to 400 kJ? [223.5 rev/min]

10 A pump delivers water of density 1000 kg/m³ through a nozzle of diameter 20 mm with a velocity of 40 m/s. Find the mass of water discharged per second through the nozzle and thus the kinetic energy per second in the water.   [12.57 kg/s; 10.056 kJ]

11 A chain connecting two wheels is 4 m long and has a mass of 2 kg per metre length. The smaller driving wheel is 0.4 m diameter and has a moment of inertia of 15 kg m^2, while the moment of inertia of the larger driven wheel is 18 kgm^2. If the speed ratio is 3:2, determine the speed of the driving wheel when the total kinetic energy in the system is 11.51 kJ. What is the linear speed of the chain?   [300 rev/min; 6.284 m/s]

12 The power required to accelerate a flywheel uniformly from rest to its running speed of 300 rev/min in 4 seconds is 5 kW. Determine (a) the uniform acceleration, (b) the accelerating torque, (c) the moment of inertia of the flywheel, (d) the kinetic energy in the flywheel when it is rotating at 300 rev/min.   [7.855 rad/s^2; 318.3 Nm; 40.52 kgm^2; 20 kJ]

13 The total mass of a waggon is 2.5 tonne, of which the mass of each wheel is 0.25 tonne. Each wheel has a diameter of 0.7 m and a radius of gyration of 0.3 m. Determine the kinetic energy in the waggon when it has a linear velocity of 18 m/s.   [524 kJ]

14 A lift cage of mass 750 kg is raised by a cable wrapped around a winding drum 2.4 m in diameter. The cage is accelerated uniformly from rest at the rate of 3 m/s^2 for 5 seconds. Determine the tension in the cable during the acceleration period.

If the winding drum has a mass of 250 kg and its radius of gyration is 0.85 m, ignoring the mass of the cable, calculate (a) the accelerating torque, (b) the total kinetic energy in the lift system after 5 seconds.
[9607.5 N; 11.98 kNm; 98.486 kJ]

15 A solid disc of mass 3.6 kg and outside diameter 150 mm is mounted on a spindle 15 mm in diameter. The spindle is in contact with two smooth parallel rails which are inclined at 7° to the horizontal. Determine the linear velocity and angular velocity of the disc when it has rolled, without slipping, 2 m along the rails. Ignore the effect of the spindle on the inertia of the disc.
[0.306 m/s; 40.8 rad/s]

6 Simple oscillations

6.1 Periodic time and frequency
An oscillation is defined as a to-and-fro motion about a mean position and is completed when the motion of M in fig. 6.1 is from O to A to B and back to O.

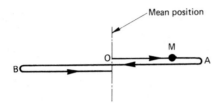

Fig. 6.1 Definition of an oscillation

The time required to complete one cycle of the motion is known as the *period* or *periodic time*, T, of the oscillation, and the number of cycles made per unit time is known as the *frequency*, f, of the oscillation. If the periodic time for each successive oscillation is the same (i.e. T), then

$$\text{frequency} = \frac{1}{\text{periodic time}}$$

or
$$f = \frac{1}{T}$$

which it is useful to remember.
The unit for frequency is the *hertz* (Hz) and for periodic time the *second* (s). It is important to note that

$$1 \text{ Hz} = 1 \text{ cycle/second} \quad \text{or} \quad 1 \text{ oscillation/second}$$
$$\text{or} \quad 1 \text{ revolution/second}$$

6.2 Displacement and amplitude
In oscillatory motion, the *displacement, x,* is measured outwards from either side of the mean position, as shown in fig. 6.2. The maximum displacement on either side of the mean position is known as the *amplitude* of the motion.

117

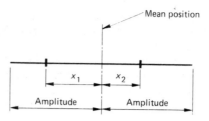

Fig. 6.2 Measurement of displacement and amplitude

6.3 Simple harmonic motion

The most common form of oscillatory motion is *simple harmonic motion* (S.H.M.). An oscillating body will have S.H.M. if, at any instant during the cycle,

i) the acceleration of the body is proportional to its displacement from the mean position, *and*

ii) the acceleration of the body is *always directed towards* the mean position.

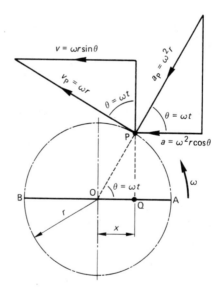

Fig. 6.3 Simple harmonic motion

Consider the motion of Q, which is the projection of P on to the line AB in fig. 6.3. P is rotating in a circle of radius r with uniform angular velocity ω, causing Q to oscillate between A and B about the mean position O. In the position shown, where P has rotated through angle θ in time t, i.e. $\theta = \omega t$,

i) the displacement of Q is $\quad x = r \cos \theta = r \cos \omega t$
ii) the horizontal component of the tangential velocity of P relative to O is
the velocity of Q towards O;
i.e. the velocity of Q towards O is $\quad v = -\omega r \sin \theta = -\omega r \sin \omega t$
The minus sign indicates that the velocity is *increasing* while the
displacement is *decreasing*. Notice that, as Q moves from O to B, the
velocity is *decreasing* and the displacement is *increasing*.

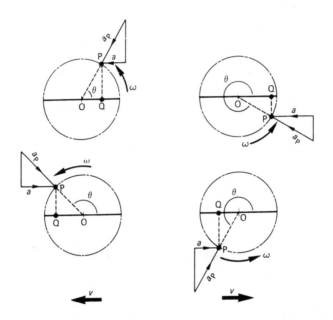

Fig. 6.4   Effect of θ on direction of velocity and acceleration

iii) the horizontal component of the *centripetal* acceleration of P towards O
is the acceleration of Q and is *always* directed towards O (see fig. 6.4);
i.e. the acceleration of Q towards O is
$$a = -\omega^2 r \cos \theta = -\omega^2 r \cos \omega t = -\omega^2 x$$
The minus sign indicates that the acceleration is *always* in the opposite
direction to the displacement.

Thus, after any time t,

displacement $x = r \cos \omega t$ $\qquad\qquad\qquad\qquad\qquad$ (i)

velocity $\quad v = \dfrac{dx}{dt} = -\omega r \sin \omega t$ $\qquad\qquad\qquad$ (ii)

acceleration $a = \dfrac{dv}{dt} = -\omega^2 r \cos \omega t = -\omega^2 x$ $\qquad$ (iii)

119

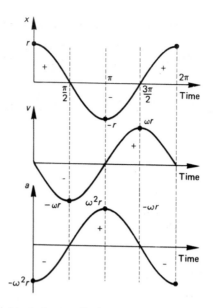

Fig. 6.5   Relationship between displacement, velocity, and acceleration

These equations, *which should be remembered*, are illustrated in the graphs of fig. 6.5.

In equation (iii), the term $-\omega^2$ is constant; therefore

$$\text{acceleration of Q towards O} = \text{constant} \times \text{displacement from O}$$

i.e. the acceleration of Q is proportional to its displacement from the mean position O and is always directed towards O; thus, Q is oscillating between A and B with *simple harmonic motion*. Notice that the constant is the square of the angular velocity of P.

Q will make one complete oscillation when P has rotated through 2π radians with an angular velocity ω,

$\therefore$ periodic time $T = \dfrac{2\pi}{\omega}$

which should be remembered.

The frequency of the oscillation of Q is

$$f = \frac{1}{T} = \frac{\omega}{2\pi}$$

which it is useful to remember.

Example 1   The amplitude of motion of a body oscillating with simple harmonic motion is 0.1 m. If the maximum velocity is 4 m/s, determine the periodic time and the frequency of the oscillation.

$v = -\omega r \sin \omega t$ and has a maximum value when $\sin \omega t = 1$

(the minus sign indicates that the velocity is opposite in direction to the displacement — for calculation purposes it may be ignored)

$\therefore$ $\omega = v_{max.}/r$

where $v_{max.} = 4$ m/s   and $r = 0.1$ m, i.e. the amplitude of the motion

$\therefore$ $\omega = \dfrac{4 \text{ m/s}}{0.1 \text{ m}}$

     $= 40$ rad/s

Periodic time $T = 2\pi/\omega$

$$= \frac{2\pi \text{ rad}}{40 \text{ rad/s}}$$

$$= 0.157 \text{ s}$$

i.e. the periodic time is 0.157 s.

Frequency $f = 1/T$

$$= \frac{1}{0.157 \text{ s}}$$

$$= 6.37 \text{ Hz}$$

i.e. the frequency is 6.37 Hz.

Example 2   A body oscillating with simple harmonic motion has an amplitude of 1.2 m and a periodic time of 5 seconds. Determine the time required for the body to move 0.5 m from its outermost position. What will be the velocity of the body at this point?

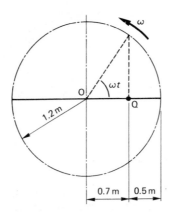

Fig. 6.6

121

The problem is shown diagrammatically in fig. 6.6.

Periodic time $T = 2\pi/\omega = 5$ s

$$\therefore \quad \omega = \frac{2\pi \text{ rad}}{5 \text{ s}}$$

$$= 1.26 \text{ rad/s}$$

From fig. 6.6,

$$\cos \omega t = \frac{0.7 \text{ m}}{1.2 \text{ m}} = 0.5833$$

$$\therefore \qquad \omega t = 54.32° = 0.948 \text{ rad}$$

$$\therefore \qquad t = \frac{0.948 \text{ rad}}{1.26 \text{ rad/s}}$$

$$= 0.75 \text{ s}$$

i.e. the time is 0.75 s.

$$v = \omega r \sin \omega t \quad \text{(ignoring the sign)}$$

$$= 1.26 \text{ rad/s} \times 1.2 \text{ m} \times \sin 54.32°$$

$$= 1.228 \text{ m/s}$$

i.e. the velocity is 1.228 m/s.

Example 3 The total movement of a body oscillating with simple harmonic motion is 150 mm. If the frequency of the oscillation is 8 Hz, determine the maximum velocity and the maximum acceleration of the body.

Since the total movement is 150 mm, the amplitude of the motion is 75 mm or 0.075 m, as shown in fig. 6.7.

Fig. 6.7

122

Frequency $f = \omega/2\pi = 8\,\text{Hz}$

$\therefore \quad \omega = 2\pi \text{ rad} \times 8\,\text{Hz}$

$\qquad = 50.27\,\text{rad/s}$

$v = \omega r \sin \omega t$ (ignoring the sign) and has a maximum value when $\sin \omega t = 1$

and $r = 0.075\,\text{m}$

$\therefore \quad v_{\text{max.}} = 50.27\,\text{rad/s} \times 0.075\,\text{m}$

$\qquad\quad = 3.77\,\text{m/s}$

i.e. the maximum velocity is 3.77 m/s.

$a = -\omega^2 r \cos \omega t$ and has a maximum value when $\cos \omega t = 1$

(the minus sign indicates that the acceleration is always in the opposite direction to the displacement — for calculation purposes it may be ignored)

$\therefore \quad a_{\text{max.}} = \omega^2 r$

$\qquad\quad = (50.27\,\text{rad/s})^2 \times 0.075\,\text{m}$

$\qquad\quad = 189.5\,\text{m/s}^2$

i.e. the maximum acceleration is 189.5 m/s² and is towards the mean position.

6.4 Free linear oscillations of a mass on a vertical spring

The spring shown in fig. 6.8(a) is of negligible mass and is assumed to obey Hooke's law, i.e. the extension of the spring is proportional to the applied force within the elastic limit.

Let a mass m be attached to the lower end of the spring, causing it to extend an amount δ. In the equilibrium position, fig. 6.8(b),

$$\text{downward force exerted by the mass} = \text{upward restoring force in the spring}$$

i.e. $mg = k\delta$

where k = spring stiffness, with units newtons per metre (N/m).

If the mass is now moved downwards through a vertical distance x from the equilibrium position, the net force acting on the mass will be as shown in fig. 6.8(c),

i.e.   net force $= mg - (kx + k\delta)$

$\qquad\qquad\qquad = k\delta - kx - k\delta$

$\qquad\qquad\qquad = -kx$

i.e. the net force acting on the mass is directly proportional to the displacement of the mass from the equilibrium position. The minus sign

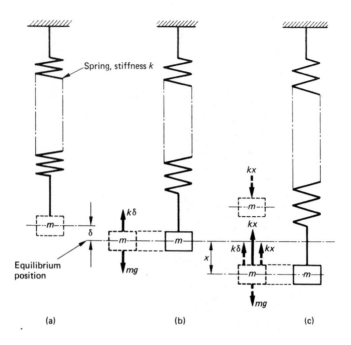

Fig. 6.8   Oscillating spring

indicates that the net force is acting towards the equilibrium position and in the opposite direction to the displacement.

If the mass is now released, it will oscillate in a vertical plane about the equilibrium position. From Newton's second law of motion, the net force will accelerate the mass in the direction of the force, i.e. towards the equilibrium position. Thus,

net force = mass x acceleration

i.e. $-kx = ma$

or $a = -\dfrac{k}{m}x$

which compares with $a = -\omega^2 x$ (equation (iii) in section 6.3);

i.e. the mass is oscillating about the equilibrium position with simple harmonic motion. Thus,

$$a = -\frac{k}{m}x = -\omega^2 x$$

or $\omega^2 = \dfrac{k}{m}$

$$\therefore \quad \omega = \sqrt{\frac{k}{m}} = \sqrt{\frac{\text{stiffness}}{\text{mass}}}$$

and periodic time $T = \dfrac{2\pi}{\omega} = 2\pi\sqrt{\dfrac{m}{k}}$

which should be remembered.

Frequency $f = \dfrac{1}{T} = \dfrac{1}{2\pi}\sqrt{\dfrac{k}{m}}$

which should be remembered.

This frequency is known as the *natural frequency of vibration* of the spring-mass system.

In the equilibrium position,

$$mg = k\delta$$

$$\therefore \quad k = \frac{mg}{\delta}$$

$\therefore$ natural frequency of vibration $f = \dfrac{1}{2\pi}\sqrt{\dfrac{mg}{m\delta}}$

or
$$f = \frac{1}{2\pi}\sqrt{\frac{g}{\delta}}$$

which it is useful to remember.

If the mass of the spring (m_s) is not negligible, then one third of this mass is added to the oscillating mass m;

$$\therefore \quad f = \frac{1}{2\pi}\sqrt{\frac{k}{m + m_s/3}}$$

which it is useful to remember. (The proof of this is beyond the scope of this book.)

Example 1 The static deflection of a spring supporting a mass is 15 mm. Determine the natural frequency of vibration of the spring–mass system.

$$f = \frac{1}{2\pi}\sqrt{\frac{g}{\delta}}$$

where $g = 9.81\text{ m/s}^2$ and $\delta = 15\text{ mm} = 0.015\text{ m}$

$$\therefore \quad f = \frac{1}{2\pi}\sqrt{\frac{9.81\text{ m/s}^2}{0.015\text{ m}}}$$

$$= 4.07\text{ Hz}$$

i.e. the natural frequency of vibration is 4.07 Hz.

Example 2 A spring of stiffness 2 kN/m and supporting a mass of 8 kg oscillates freely with an amplitude of vibration of 18 mm. Determine the frequency of the vibration and the velocity of the mass when it is 6 mm from the equilibrium position.

$$f = \frac{1}{2\pi} \sqrt{\frac{k}{m}}$$

where $k = 2\,\text{kN/m} = 2 \times 10^3\,\text{N/m}$ and $m = 8\,\text{kg}$

$$\therefore \quad f = \frac{1}{2\pi} \sqrt{\frac{2 \times 10^3\,\text{N/m}}{8\,\text{kg}}}$$

$$= 2.52\,\text{Hz}$$

i.e. the frequency is 2.52 Hz.

From section 6.3,

$$v = \omega r \sin \omega t \quad \text{(ignoring the sign)}$$

where $\omega = \sqrt{(k/m)} = 15.81\,\text{rad/s}$ and $r = 18\,\text{mm} = 0.018\,\text{m}$

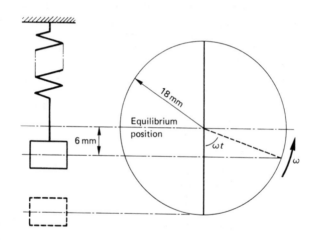

Fig. 6.9

From fig. 6.9,

$$\cos \omega t = \frac{6\,\text{mm}}{18\,\text{mm}} = 0.333$$

$$\therefore \quad \omega t = 70.53°$$

$$\therefore \quad v = 15.81\,\text{rad/s} \times 0.018\,\text{m} \times \sin 70.53°$$

$$= 0.268\,\text{m/s}$$

i.e. the velocity when the mass is 6 mm from the equilibrium position is 0.268 m/s.

Example 3 A spring of mass 6 kg oscillates with a frequency of 5 Hz when supporting a mass of 20 kg. What is the stiffness of the spring?

$$f = \frac{1}{2\pi} \sqrt{\frac{k}{m + m_s/3}}$$

∴ $k = (2\pi f)^2 (m + m_s/3)$

where $f = 5\,\text{Hz}$ $m = 20\,\text{kg}$ and $m_s = 6\,\text{kg}$

∴ $k = (2\pi\,\text{rad} \times 5\,\text{Hz})^2\,[20\,\text{kg} + (6\,\text{kg})/3]$

       $= 21.7 \times 10^3\,\text{N/m}$ or $21.7\,\text{kN/m}$

i.e. the stiffness is $21.7\,\text{kN/m}$.

6.5 Oscillations of a simple pendulum

A simple pendulum is a concentrated mass suspended from a fixed point by a string which is assumed to have no mass and which will not stretch. Figure 6.10(a) shows a simple pendulum oscillating between OA and OB. At the instant shown, the angular displacement from the mean position OC is θ radians and the linear displacement of the mass from C is x. The downward force mg being exerted by the mass can be resolved into two perpendicular components as shown in fig. 6.10(b).

Referring to fig. 6.10(b), the perpendicular components of mg are

i) the tension in the string
   i.e. $mg \cos \theta$

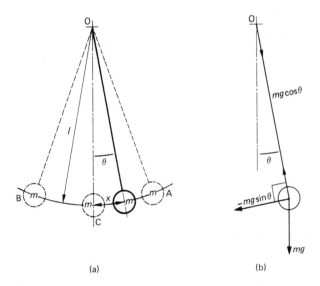

(a)   (b)

Fig. 6.10 Simple pendulum

ii) the tangential force in the direction of the mean position OC

    i.e. $-mg \sin \theta$

The minus sign indicates that the force is acting in the opposite direction to the displacement for *all* positions of the pendulum between OA and OB.

The tension in the string has no effect on the motion and is thus ignored. The tangential force in the direction of OC will produce an acceleration which is *always* directed towards the mean position.

From Newton's second law of motion,

i.e.   force = mass × acceleration

$$-mg \sin \theta = ma$$

or $a = -g \sin \theta$

For small values of θ, typically less than $10°$,

$$\sin \theta \approx x/l$$

$\therefore$ $a = -\dfrac{g}{l} x$

which compares with $a = -\omega^2 x$ (equation (iii) in section 6.3);

i.e. the pendulum is oscillating between OA and OB with simple harmonic motion. Thus,

$$a = -\frac{g}{l} x = -\omega^2 x$$

or $\omega^2 = \dfrac{g}{l}$

$\therefore$ $\omega = \sqrt{\dfrac{g}{l}}$

and   periodic time $T = \dfrac{2\pi}{\omega} = 2\pi \sqrt{\dfrac{l}{g}}$

which should be remembered.

    Frequency $f = \dfrac{1}{T} = \dfrac{1}{2\pi} \sqrt{\dfrac{g}{l}}$

which should be remembered.

This frequency is also known as the natural frequency of oscillation of a simple pendulum. Notice that the periodic time and the natural frequency of oscillation of a simple pendulum are independent of the mass. It should be noted that the above equations are valid only for small amplitudes of motion, typically less than $10°$.

Example 1   Determine the frequency and periodic time of a simple pendulum of length 1.3 m.

Frequency $f = \dfrac{1}{2\pi} \sqrt{\dfrac{g}{l}}$

where $g = 9.81 \text{ m/s}^2$ and $l = 1.3 \text{ m}$

$\therefore \quad f = \dfrac{1}{2\pi} \sqrt{\dfrac{9.81 \text{ m/s}^2}{1.3 \text{ m}}}$

$= 0.437 \text{ Hz}$

i.e. the frequency is 0.437 Hz.

Periodic time $T = 1/f$

$= \dfrac{1}{0.437 \text{ Hz}}$

$= 2.29 \text{ s}$

i.e. the periodic time is 2.29 seconds.

Example 2 A simple pendulum is oscillating with an amplitude of 6°. If the pendulum is 0.9 m long, determine (a) the periodic time, (b) the maximum angular velocity, (c) the maximum angular acceleration.

a) $T = 2\pi \sqrt{(l/g)}$

where $l = 0.9 \text{ m}$ and $g = 9.81 \text{ m/s}^2$

$\therefore \quad T = 2\pi \text{ rad} \sqrt{\dfrac{0.9 \text{ m}}{9.81 \text{ m/s}^2}}$

$= 1.9 \text{ s}$

i.e. the periodic time is 1.9 seconds.

b) From section 6.3 and ignoring the sign,

$v_{\text{max.}} = \omega r$

Let Ω = maximum angular velocity of the pendulum about O; then, for a simple pendulum of length l,

$\Omega = \dfrac{v_{\text{max.}}}{l} = \dfrac{\omega r}{l}$

But $r/l = \theta$ (the maximum angular displacement)

$\therefore \quad \Omega = \omega\theta$

which it is useful to remember.

Here $\omega = \dfrac{2\pi}{T} = \dfrac{2\pi \text{ rad}}{1.9 \text{ s}} = 3.31 \text{ rad/s}$ and $\theta = 6° = 0.105 \text{ rad}$

$\therefore \quad \Omega = 3.31 \text{ rad/s} \times 0.105 \text{ rad}$

$\qquad = 0.348 \text{ rad/s}$

i.e. the maximum angular velocity is 0.348 rad/s.

c) From section 6.3 and ignoring the sign,

$$a_{max.} = \omega^2 r$$

Let α = the maximum angular acceleration of the pendulum about O; then, for a simple pendulum of length l,

$$\alpha = a_{max.}/l = \omega^2 r/l$$

As before, $\quad r/l = \theta$

$\therefore \quad \alpha = \omega^2 \theta$

which it is useful to remember.

$\therefore \quad \alpha = (3.31 \text{ rad/s})^2 \times 0.105 \text{ rad}$

$\qquad = 1.15 \text{ rad/s}^2$

i.e. the maximum angular acceleration is 1.15 rad/s^2.

6.6 Resonance

All solid matter has a natural frequency of vibration. This frequency is determined by:

i) the density of the material — the greater the density, the higher the natural frequency of vibration;
ii) the shape of the material — long slender objects have a lower natural frequency of vibration than short stocky objects.

Objects will vibrate at their natural frequency of vibration if, as with the spring–mass system in section 6.4, an external force is applied which disturbs the equilibrium of the system. This external force is known as a *disturbing force*.

In the spring–mass system of section 6.4, the disturbing force was provided by moving the mass downwards, thus extending the spring. On release, the mass oscillated in a vertical plane, each succeeding amplitude of motion getting smaller until the vibration died away. If the disturbing force could be applied with a frequency equal to the natural frequency of vibration of the system — i.e. every time the mass moved down, an external force acted on it — the amplitude of the motion would get larger and larger until the spring was stretched beyond its elastic limit and eventually to failure. When the mass is vibrating in such a way, the system is said to be in *resonance* and the mass is *resonating*; i.e. *resonance will occur when the frequency of the external disturbing force is equal to the natural frequency of vibration of the system,* which should be remembered.

Resonance conditions usually occur in machines or other devices which have rotating parts. For example, when machining an awkwardly shaped casting on a lathe, it is not usually possible to achieve perfect rotational balance; thus, with every revolution of the spindle, an out-of-balance disturbing force is imparted through the lathe structure to its foundations. As the speed of rotation approaches the natural frequency of vibration of the foundation, the lathe will resonate. The effect of the resonance will clearly be seen, both in the machine-tool structure and in the poor surface finish obtained on the workpiece. Other examples include high-speed domestic spin-dryers — as the spin tub increases speed, it will invariably pass through a speed equal to the natural frequency of vibration of the tub's elastic mounting, causing it to vibrate violently for several seconds. An unbalanced car wheel will cause the vehicle to resonate when the wheel rotates at a speed equal to the natural frequency of vibration of the suspension system — this is recognised by the sudden increase in noise heard within the body of the car.

Exercises on chapter 6

1   A body moves with simple harmonic motion between two points 600 mm apart. Its velocity when passing through the mid-point is 6 m/s. Determine the periodic time and the frequency of the oscillation.   [0.314 s; 3.18 Hz]

2   The amplitude of a body oscillating with simple harmonic motion is 200 mm. If the periodic time for the oscillation is 1.4 seconds, determine the maximum velocity and the maximum acceleration of the body.
[0.9 m/s; 4.03 m/s^2]

3   The maximum acceleration and periodic time of a body moving with simple harmonic motion are 5.86 m/s^2 and 0.8 seconds respectively. Determine the amplitude of the motion and the maximum velocity.
[95 mm; 0.75 m/s]

4   If the frequency of a body oscillating with simple harmonic motion is 3 Hz and the amplitude of the motion is 60 mm, determine the velocity and acceleration of the body when it is at a point midway between the maximum displacement and the mean position.   [0.98 m/s; 10.66 m/s^2]

5   When a body oscillating with simple harmonic motion is 20 mm from the mean position, its velocity and acceleration are 4 m/s and 1.8 m/s^2 respectively. For the motion, determine the periodic time, the amplitude, and the maximum acceleration.   [0.662 s; 0.422 m; 38 m/s^2]

6   Define simple harmonic motion.
   A body moving with simple harmonic motion has a maximum velocity and acceleration of 5 m/s and 3 m/s^2 respectively. Determine the amplitude, frequency, and periodic time of the oscillation.   [8.33 m; 0.095 Hz; 10.47 s]

7   The static deflection at the foundation of a machine tool was 2.7 mm. Determine the natural frequency of vibration of the foundation.   [9.6 Hz]

8   A spring deflects 3 mm when supporting a mass of 6 kg. Determine the natural frequency of vibration and the periodic time when the spring is supporting a mass of 8 kg.   [7.88 Hz; 0.127 s]

9   Determine the natural frequency of vibration when a spring of stiffness 15 kN/m supports a mass of 40 kg.   [3.08 Hz]

10 A spring has a mass of 10 kg and a stiffness of 12 kN/m. If, when supporting a mass, the natural frequency of vibration is 5 Hz, determine the magnitude of the mass.   [8.825 kg]

11 A spring–mass system has a periodic time of 0.3 seconds when oscillating at its natural frequency. If the mass is 15 kg, determine the spring stiffness. [6.58 kN/m]

12 Show that a spring supporting a mass will oscillate in a vertical plane with simple harmonic motion.

A spring of stiffness 35 kN/m has a natural frequency of vibration of 6 Hz when supporting a mass of 20 kg. What is the mass of the spring?   [13.9 kg]

13 A spring of stiffness 20 kN/m and supporting a mass of 5 kg has an amplitude of motion of 20 mm. For the mass, determine (a) its maximum velocity and acceleration, (b) its velocity and acceleration at a point 4 mm from the outermost position.   [1.26 m/s, 80 m/s^2; 0.75 m/s, 64 m/s^2]

14 A simple pendulum is 1.1 m long. What are its periodic time and natural frequency of oscillation?   [2.1 s; 0.476 Hz]

15 Show that a simple pendulum oscillates freely with simple harmonic motion.

A simple pendulum of length 0.8 m has an amplitude of motion of 5°. Determine the maximum angular velocity and angular acceleration of the bob. [0.306 rad/s; 1.07 rad/s^2]

16 The amplitude of motion of a simple pendulum is 8°, and when it is 4° from the mean position its velocity is 0.8 m/s. Determine the length of the pendulum and the periodic time of the oscillation.   [4.44 m; 4.22 s]

17 Explain the meaning of the term 'resonance' as applied to a system which may oscillate, and give *two* examples where resonance may occur.

18 Describe how resonance in a domestic spin-drying machine could be overcome.

19 A body of mass 10 kg oscillates in a straight line with simple harmonic motion. When the body is displaced 0.4 m from the central position of its motion, its velocity and acceleration are 5 m/s and 30 m/s^2 respectively. Determine (a) the frequency of the oscillation, (b) the amplitude of the oscillation, (c) the maximum velocity, (d) the maximum force acting on the body.   [1.38 Hz; 0.733 m; 6.35 m/s; 550 N]

7 Fluids in motion

7.1 Introduction
Any liquid fluid which is in motion contains energy by virtue of its pressure and density (pressure energy), velocity (kinetic energy), and its position relative to some datum (potential energy).

7.2 Pressure energy
Let the mass of fluid between X and Y in fig. 7.1 have a total volume V_1. For flow to occur, this volume must be displaced by an equal volume entering from outside the system. If the pressure in the fluid is p_1, then the work done on the fluid *inside* the system by the incoming fluid is equal to force x distance s the fluid is displaced.

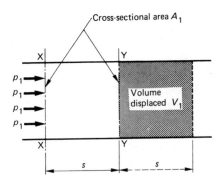

Fig. 7.1   Pressure energy

But   force = pressure x cross-sectional area = $p_1 A_1$

$\therefore$ work done = $p_1 A_1 s$

But $A_1 s$ = volume displaced, V_1

$\therefore$ work done on the system = $p_1 V_1$

i.e. the incoming fluid increases the energy in the system by an amount $p_1 V_1$. This energy is known as *pressure energy* or *flow work energy*.

Similarly, the fluid leaving the system will do work equal to $p_2 V_2$ on the surroundings; i.e. the outgoing fluid reduces the energy in the system by an amount $p_2 V_2$, where p_2 and V_2 represent respectively the pressure and volume at exit from the system.

If the mass of fluid occupying volume V_1 is m_1, the mass occupying volume V_2 is m_2, and the density of the fluid is ρ (*rho*), then

$$\rho = \frac{m_1}{V_1} = \frac{m_2}{V_2}$$

Thus,   at point 1 in the system, the *specific* pressure energy $= \dfrac{p_1}{\rho}$

and   at point 2 in the system, the *specific* pressure energy $= \dfrac{p_2}{\rho}$

which should be remembered.

The term *specific energy* means energy per unit mass of fluid. The units for specific pressure energy are joules per kilogram (J/kg).

7.3 Kinetic energy

If a mass m of fluid has a linear velocity v, then

kinetic energy in the fluid $= \frac{1}{2}mv^2$

For unit mass of fluid,

specific kinetic energy $= \frac{1}{2}v^2$

which it is useful to remember.

7.4 Potential energy

If a mass m of fluid is stored at a height h above the datum, then

potential energy stored in the fluid $= mgh$

For unit mass of fluid,

specific potential energy $= gh$

which it is useful to remember.

7.5 Bernoulli's equation

Let unit mass of fluid flow at a steady rate through the system shown in fig. 7.2. Applying the principle of conservation of energy,

i.e.   specific energy in the fluid entering the system $=$ specific energy in the fluid leaving the system

or   specific pressure energy $+$ specific kinetic energy $+$ specific potential energy $=$ specific pressure energy $+$ specific kinetic energy $+$ specific potential energy

at entry   at exit

$$\therefore \quad \frac{p_1}{\rho} + \frac{v_1^2}{2} + gh_1 = \frac{p_2}{\rho} + \frac{v_2^2}{2} + gh_2 = \text{constant}$$

134

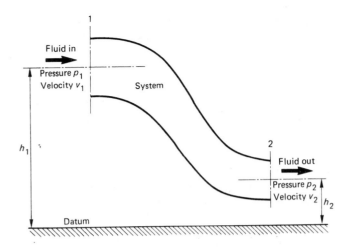

Fig. 7.2 Bernoulli's equation

Dividing both sides of the equation by g,

$$\frac{p_1}{\rho g} + \frac{v_1^2}{2g} + h_1 = \frac{p_2}{\rho g} + \frac{v_2^2}{2g} + h_2 = \text{constant}$$

This is known as Bernoulli's equation and should be remembered.

Each quantity in the Bernoulli equation is measured in terms of 'head of liquid', i.e. height of liquid above a given datum. The unit for each quantity is the *metre* (m).

Example   Water enters a pipeline with a pressure of 2 bar and velocity 5 m/s. If the pressure in the water 25 m below the entry point is 1.2 bar, calculate the velocity. Take the density of water as 1000 kg/m³.

Using Bernoulli's equation,

i.e. $\dfrac{p_1}{\rho g} + \dfrac{v_1^2}{2g} + h_1 = \dfrac{p_2}{\rho g} + \dfrac{v_2^2}{2g} + h_2$

gives $v_2 = \sqrt{\left(v_1^2 + \dfrac{2(p_1 - p_2)}{\rho} + (h_1 - h_2)2g \right)}$

For convenience, make the point 25 m below the entry point the datum,

i.e. $h_2 = 0$ and $h_1 = 25\,\text{m}$

Also, $v_1 = 5\,\text{m/s}$ $p_1 = 2\,\text{bar} = 2 \times 10^5\,\text{N/m}^2$

$p_2 = 1.2\,\text{bar} = 1.2 \times 10^5\,\text{N/m}^2$ $g = 9.81\,\text{m/s}^2$

and $\rho = 1000\,\text{kg/m}^3$

135

$$\therefore v_2 = \sqrt{\left((5 \text{ m/s})^2 + \frac{2(2 - 1.2) \times 10^5 \text{ N/m}^2}{1000 \text{ kg/m}^3} + (25 \text{ m} - 0) \times 2 \times 9.81 \text{ m/s}^2\right)}$$

$$= \sqrt{(25 + 490.5 + 160)} \text{ m/s}$$

$$= 26 \text{ m/s}$$

i.e. the velocity of the water is 26 m/s.

7.6 Frictional resistance to flow

Bernoulli's equation assumes there to be no frictional resistance to the flow. In practice, frictional resistance to flow is *always* present and reduces the available energy in the fluid at exit from the system;

i.e.   specific energy   specific energy   specific energy to
       in fluid entering = in fluid leaving + overcome frictional
       the system   the system   resistance to flow

Let h_f = frictional resistance 'head'

then $\dfrac{p_1}{\rho g} + \dfrac{v_1^2}{2g} + h_1 = \dfrac{p_2}{\rho g} + \dfrac{v_2^2}{2g} + h_2 + h_f$

which it is useful to remember.

Example   Water of density 1000 kg/m³ enters a horizontal pipeline with a pressure and velocity of 2 MPa and 7.5 m/s respectively, and leaves with a pressure of 1.65 MPa and velocity 25 m/s. Determine the loss of head due to frictional resistance.

Frictional resistance head = energy input head − energy output head

or $h_f = \dfrac{(p_1 - p_2)}{\rho g} + \dfrac{(v_1^2 - v_2^2)}{2g} + (h_1 - h_2)$

where $p_1 = 2 \text{ MPa} = 2 \times 10^6 \text{ N/m}^2$ $p_2 = 1.65 \text{ MPa} = 1.65 \times 10^6 \text{ N/m}^2$

$\rho = 1000 \text{ kg/m}^3$ $g = 9.81 \text{ m/s}^2$ $v_1 = 7.5 \text{ m/s}$

and $v_2 = 25 \text{ m/s}$

Since the pipeline is horizontal, $h_1 = h_2 = 0$

$$\therefore \quad h_f = \frac{(2 - 1.65) \times 10^6 \text{ N/m}^2}{1000 \text{ kg/m}^3 \times 9.81 \text{ m/s}^2} + \frac{(7.5^2 - 25^2) \, (\text{m/s})^2}{2 \times 9.81 \text{ m/s}^2} + 0$$

$$= 35.68 \text{ m} + (-29 \text{ m})$$

$$= 6.68 \text{ m}$$

i.e. the loss of head due to friction is 6.68 m.

7.7 Continuity equation

Consider sections 1 and 2 in the tapered pipe shown in fig. 7.3, which is full of steadily flowing fluid. At section 1, the cross-sectional area is A_1 and the velocity of the fluid is v_1; at section 2, the area and velocity are A_2 and v_2 respectively.

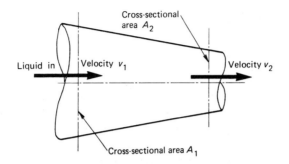

Fig. 7.3   Continuity equation

Since the pipe is full of fluid and the flow is steady, then, applying the principle of conservation of matter,

mass of fluid passing   =   mass of fluid passing
section 1 per unit time   section 2 per unit time

i.e. $\dot{m}_1 = \dot{m}_2$

where $\dot{m}$ = mass flow rate in kilograms per second (kg/s)

But   mass flow rate = density x cross-sectional area x velocity = $\rho A v$

∴ $\rho_1 A_1 v_1 = \rho_2 A_2 v_2$

This is known as the continuity equation for steady flow, and should be remembered.

If the density ρ remains constant, then

$$A_1 v_1 = A_2 v_2$$

If at sections 1 and 2 the pipe is circular with diameters d_1 and d_2 respectively, then

$$\frac{\pi}{4} d_1^2 v_1 = \frac{\pi}{4} d_2^2 v_2$$

or $d_1^2 v_1 = d_2^2 v_2$

which it is useful to remember.

Example   At a section in a tapered pipe, the diameter is 0.7 m and the velocity of the liquid is 5 m/s. Assuming the flow of the fluid to be steady, determine the velocity when the pipe diameter is 0.5 m.

Since the pipe is circular,

$$d_1^2 v_1 = d_2^2 v_2$$

$$\therefore \quad v_2 = (d_1/d_2)^2 v_1$$

where $d_1 = 0.7$ m $\quad d_2 = 0.5$ m $\quad$ and $\quad v_1 = 5$ m/s

$$\therefore \quad v_2 = \left(\frac{0.7 \text{ m}}{0.5 \text{ m}}\right)^2 \times 5 \text{ m/s}$$

$$= 9.8 \text{ m/s}$$

i.e. the velocity is 9.8 m/s.

7.8 Applications of the Bernoulli and continuity equations

Example 1   Oil of density 800 kg/m³ enters a 500 mm diameter pipeline with a velocity of 3 m/s and pressure 400 kPa, and is discharged through an orifice 150 mm in diameter and 30 m below the entry point. If the frictional losses are equivalent to a head of 3.5 m of the oil, determine the velocity and pressure of the oil at the point of discharge.

To find the velocity, use the continuity equation for a circular pipe,

i.e. $\quad d_1^2 v_1 = d_2^2 v_2$

$$\therefore \quad v_2 = (d_1/d_2)^2 v_1$$

where $d_1 = 500$ mm $\quad d_2 = 150$ mm $\quad$ and $\quad v_1 = 3$ m/s

$$\therefore \quad v_2 = \left(\frac{500 \text{ mm}}{150 \text{ mm}}\right)^2 \times 3 \text{ m/s}$$

$$= 33.3 \text{ m/s}$$

i.e. the velocity at discharge is 33.3 m/s.

To find the pressure, use Bernoulli's equation,

i.e. $\quad \dfrac{p_1}{\rho g} + \dfrac{v_1^2}{2g} + h_1 = \dfrac{p_2}{\rho g} + \dfrac{v_2^2}{2g} + h_2 + h_f$

$$\therefore \quad p_2 = p_1 + \tfrac{1}{2}(v_1^2 - v_2^2)\rho + (h_1 - h_2 - h_f)\rho g$$

where $p_1 = 400$ kPa $= 400 \times 10^3$ N/m² $\quad v_1 = 3$ m/s

$\qquad\qquad v_2 = 33.3$ m/s $\qquad \rho = 800$ kg/m³ $\qquad g = 9.81$ m/s²

$\qquad\qquad h_f = 3.5$ m $\quad$ and, making the orifice the datum, $\quad h_2 = 0$

and $\qquad h_1 = 30$ m

$$p_2 = [400 \times 10^3 \, \text{N/m}^2] + [\tfrac{1}{2}(3^2 - 33.3^2)(\text{m/s})^2 \times 800 \, \text{kg/m}^3]$$
$$\qquad + [(30 - 0 - 3.5)\text{m} \times 9.81 \, \text{m/s}^2 \times 800 \, \text{kg/m}^3]$$
$$= [400 \times 10^3 \, \text{N/m}^2] + [-440 \times 10^3 \, \text{N/m}^2] + [208 \times 10^3 \, \text{N/m}^2]$$
$$= 168 \times 10^3 \, \text{N/m}^2 \quad \text{or} \quad 168 \, \text{kPa}$$

i.e. the pressure at discharge is 168 kPa.

Example 2   Water contained in an open tank is discharged to the atmosphere through an orifice 25 mm in diameter. If the surface of the water is maintained at a constant 1.6 m above the centre of the orifice, and ignoring losses, determine (a) the velocity of the water as it discharges through the orifice, (b) the volume of water flowing in litres per minute.

a) Referring to fig. 7.4 and applying Bernoulli's equation,

$$\frac{p_1}{\rho g} + \frac{v_1^2}{2g} + h_1 = \frac{p_2}{\rho g} + \frac{v_2^2}{2g} + h_2 + h_f$$

Putting the datum through the centre of the orifice makes $h_2 = 0$. Also,

$$p_1 = p_2$$

$v_1 = 0$ (since there is no movement at the surface of the water)

and $h_f = 0$

$\therefore \quad h_1 = v_2^2/2g$

or $v_2 = \sqrt{2gh_1}$

where $h_1 = 1.6 \, \text{m}$ and $g = 9.81 \, \text{m/s}^2$

$\therefore \quad v_2 = \sqrt{(2 \times 9.81 \, \text{m/s}^2 \times 1.6 \, \text{m})}$

$\qquad = 5.6 \, \text{m/s}$

i.e. the velocity is 5.6 m/s.

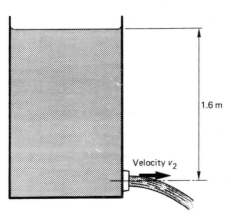

1.6 m

Velocity v_2

Fig. 7.4

b) Volume of water flowing per second = area of orifice x velocity

$$= (\pi/4) \times (0.025 \text{ m})^2 \times 5.6 \text{ m/s}$$
$$= 0.0027 \text{ m}^3/\text{s}$$

But $1 \text{ m}^3 = 1000$ litres

∴   flow rate in litres per minute $= 0.0027 \text{ m}^3/\text{s} \times 1000 \text{ 1/m}^3 \times 60 \text{ s/min}$

$$= 162 \text{ 1/min}$$

i.e. the volume of water flowing is 162 litres per minute.

Example 3   Water with a gauge pressure of 500 kPa and having negligible velocity is discharged to the atmosphere through a horizontal nozzle 20 mm in diameter. Ignoring losses, determine the velocity of discharge and the volumetric flow rate in litres per minute. The density of the water is 1000 kg/m^3.

From Bernoulli's equation,

$$\frac{p_1}{\rho g} + \frac{v_1^2}{2g} + h_1 = \frac{p_2}{\rho g} + \frac{v_2^2}{2g} + h_2 + h_f$$

Here $p_2 = 0$ $v_1 = 0$ $h_f = 0$

and $h_1 = h_2 = 0$ (since nozzle is horizontal)

∴ $p_1/\rho g = v_2^2/2g$

or $v_2 = \sqrt{(2p_1/\rho)}$

where $p_1 = 500 \text{ kPa} = 500 \times 10^3 \text{ N/m}^2$ and $\rho = 1000 \text{ kg/m}^3$

∴ $v_2 = \sqrt{\dfrac{2 \times 500 \times 10^3 \text{ N/m}^2}{1000 \text{ kg/m}^3}}$

$$= 31.62 \text{ m/s}$$

i.e. the velocity of discharge is 31.62 m/s.

Volumetric flow rate $= Av$

where $A = (\pi/4) \times (0.02 \text{ m})^2 = 0.000\,314 \text{ m}^2$

∴   volumetric flow rate $= 0.000\,314 \text{ m}^2 \times 31.62 \text{ m/s}$

$$= 0.009\,93 \text{ m}^3/\text{s}$$

$$= 596 \text{ litres/min}$$

(since $1 \text{ m}^3/\text{s} = 60 \times 10^3 \text{ litres/min}$)

i.e. the volumetric flow rate is 596 litres/min.

Example 4   The outlet pipe from a reservoir serving a hydroelectric power station is 30 m below the surface of the water. The pipe is 400 m long and is inclined at 60° to the horizontal. The outlet nozzle at the turbine is 600 mm in diameter. Taking frictional losses as equivalent to 2% of the potential head, determine (a) the pressure in the water at entry to the pipe, (b) the velocity of the water issuing from the nozzle, (c) the velocity in the pipe when its diameter is 2 m. Take the density of water as 1000 kg/m³.

a)   Pressure in the water at entry to the pipe = $\rho g h$

where ρ = 1000 kg/m³ g = 9.81 m/s²   and h = 30 m

∴   pressure = 1000 kg/m³ × 9.81 m/s² × 30 m

$\qquad\qquad$ = 294.3 × 10³ N/m²   or   294.3 kPa

i.e. the pressure at entry to the pipe is 294.3 kPa.

b)   From Bernoulli's equation,

$$\frac{p_1}{\rho g} + \frac{v_1^2}{2g} + h_1 = \frac{p_2}{\rho g} + \frac{v_2^2}{2g} + h_2 + h_f$$

Referring to fig. 7.5 and making the nozzle exit the datum,

$\qquad h_2 = 0 \qquad h_1 = (400\text{ m} \times \sin 60°) + 30\text{ m} = 376.4\text{ m}$

and h_f = 2% of h_1 = 7.53 m

Also, $p_1 = p_2$ (since the surface of the water and the exit from the nozzle are both at atmospheric pressure)   and v_1 = 0

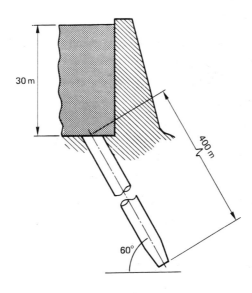

30 m

400 m

60°

Fig. 7.5

141

$\therefore$ exit velocity $v_2 = \sqrt{[2g(h_1 - h_f)]}$

$= \sqrt{[(2 \times 9.81 \text{ m/s}^2)(376.4 \text{ m} - 7.53 \text{ m})]}$

$= 85.07 \text{ m/s}$

i.e. the velocity of the water issuing from the nozzle is 85.07 m/s.

c)   Using the continuity equation for a circular pipe,

i.e. $d_1^2 v_1 = d_2^2 v_2$

$v_1 = (d_2/d_1)^2 v_2$

where $d_1 = 2 \text{ m}$ and $d_2 = 600 \text{ mm} = 0.6 \text{ m}$

$\therefore$ $v_1 = \left(\dfrac{0.6 \text{ m}}{2 \text{ m}}\right)^2 \times 85.07 \text{ m/s}$

$= 7.66 \text{ m/s}$

i.e. the velocity at the point where the pipe is 2 m diameter is 7.66 m/s.

7.9 Flow through an orifice

When fluid emerges through a sharp-edged orifice, the diameter of the ensuing jet continues to contract until it reaches its minimum value a short distance from the exit point, as shown in fig. 7.6(b). This contracted area is called the *vena contracta*.

Let A = cross-sectional area of the orifice = $(\pi/4)d^2$

and A_c = cross-sectional area of the jet at the vena contracta = $(\pi/4)d_c^2$

then $A_c = C_c A$

or $C_c = \dfrac{A_c}{A} = \left(\dfrac{d_c}{d}\right)^2$

where C_c is the *coefficient of contraction*.

(a)

Vena contracta

(b)

Fig. 7.6

142

For an orifice with a perfectly sharp edge, $C_c \approx 0.6$. As the edge of the orifice becomes less sharp, the value of C_c will increase to a maximum possible value of 1.0.

In the open-topped tank shown in fig. 7.6(a), if the surface of the fluid is maintained at a constant height h above the centre of the orifice and there are no energy losses, the velocity of the fluid at the vena contracta is

$$v_c = \sqrt{2gh}$$

As the fluid passes through the orifice, its velocity will be reduced due to friction. Thus, the *actual* velocity of the fluid at the vena contracta is

$$v = C_v v_c = C_v\sqrt{2gh}$$

or $\quad C_v = \dfrac{v}{\sqrt{(2gh)}}$

where C_v is the *coefficient of velocity*. Typically, values for C_v vary between 0.95 and 0.99.

At the vena contracta, the volumetric flow rate Q of the fluid is given by

Q = area of the jet at the vena contracta x actual velocity

$\quad = A_c v$

or $\quad Q = C_c A C_v\sqrt{2gh}$

The coefficients of contraction and velocity are usually combined to give the *coefficient of discharge*, C_d.

i.e. $\quad C_d = C_c C_v$

and $\quad Q = C_d A\sqrt{2gh}$

Typically, values for C_d vary between 0.6 and 0.65.

Values for the coefficients of discharge, contraction, and velocity may be determined experimentally using a flow tank similar to that shown in fig. 7.7. Referring to fig. 7.7, the flow of water into the open-topped tank is adjusted so that the surface of the water is at a constant height h above the centre of the orifice which is located in the vertical side of the tank. At the outlet from the orifice is a ring holding three equally spaced and pointed screws through which the ensuing jet passes – the screws can be adjusted to find the diameter of the water jet at the vena contracta. The horizontal wire at W can be adjusted both horizontally and vertically until it lies in the path of the water jet to find the values of x and y. At the end of the system is a calibrated collection tank which is used to determine the volume of water flowing per unit time. Alternatively, the water can be collected in a removable tank which can then be weighed to determine the mass of water flowing per unit time. This latter method of water collection and measurement will yield more reliable data.

Having determined values for the diameter at the vena contracta (d_c), heights h and y, horizontal distance x, and volumetric flow rate Q, the co-efficients of contraction, velocity, and discharge can be calculated as follows.

Fig. 7.7

To find C_c
$$C_c = \left(\frac{d_c}{d}\right)^2$$

where d = diameter of the orifice

To find C_v
From the equations for uniform motion, the horizontal distance x moved by a particle in the water jet in time t is given by

$$x = vt \qquad\qquad\qquad\qquad\qquad\qquad\qquad \text{(i)}$$

where v = velocity of the particle at the vena contracta

Also, the vertical distance y moved by the particle is given by

$$y = \tfrac{1}{2}gt^2$$
$$\therefore \quad t = \sqrt{2y/g}$$

Substituting for t in equation (i) gives

$$x = v\sqrt{2y/g}$$
$$\text{or} \quad v = x\sqrt{g/2y}$$
$$\therefore \quad C_v = \frac{v}{v_c} = \frac{x\sqrt{(g/2y)}}{\sqrt{(2gh)}}$$
$$\text{or} \quad C_v = \frac{x}{2\sqrt{(yh)}}$$

144

To find C_d

$$C_d = \frac{Q}{A\sqrt{(2gh)}} = \frac{\dot{m}}{\rho A\sqrt{(2gh)}}$$

where Q = volumetric flow rate

         $\dot{m}$ = mass flow rate

and ρ = density of water

It should be noted that it is only necessary to determine *any two* of the above coefficients, since the third value can be determined from the relationship $C_d = C_c C_v$.

Example   In a test on a sharp-edged orifice using the flow tank shown in fig. 7.7, the following data were obtained:

     diameter of orifice   15 mm
     height h of water above centre of orifice   1.2 m
     horizontal distance x from vena contracta   1.18 m
     vertical height y 300 mm
     duration of test   10 minutes
     volume of water collected   0.329 m³

Estimate the coefficients of velocity, discharge, and contraction.

$$C_v = \frac{x}{2\sqrt{(yh)}}$$

where $x = 1.18$ m $y = 0.3$ m   and $h = 1.2$ m

$$\therefore \ C_v = \frac{1.18 \text{m}}{2\sqrt{(0.3 \text{m} \times 1.2 \text{m})}}$$

$$= 0.98$$

i.e. the coefficient of velocity is 0.98.

$$C_d = \frac{Q}{A\sqrt{(2gh)}}$$

where $Q = \dfrac{0.329 \text{m}^3}{10 \text{min} \times 60 \text{s/min}} = 548.3 \times 10^{-6} \text{ m}^3/\text{s}$

          $A = (\pi/4) \times (0.015 \text{m})^2 = 176.7 \times 10^{-6} \text{ m}^2$

          $h = 1.2$ m   and $g = 9.81 \text{ m/s}^2$

$$\therefore \ C_d = \frac{548.3 \times 10^{-6} \text{ m}^3/\text{s}}{176.7 \times 10^{-6} \text{ m}^2 \sqrt{(2 \times 9.81 \text{m/s}^2 \times 1.2 \text{m})}}$$

$$= 0.64$$

i.e. the coefficient of discharge is 0.64.

$$C_d = C_c C_v$$

$$\therefore \quad C_c = \frac{C_d}{C_v}$$

$$= \frac{0.64}{0.98}$$

$$= 0.65$$

i.e. the coefficient of contraction is 0.65.

7.10 Effect of approach velocity on flow through an orifice

The equation for volumetric flow rate Q stated in section 7.9 assumes that the velocity at entry to the orifice is zero. Where orifice plates are inserted in pipe-lines to measure flow rate as shown in fig. 7.8, the velocity in the fluid at entry to the orifice is not zero and the equation for Q is modified to give

$$Q = K C_d A \sqrt{2gH}$$

$$= \frac{1}{\sqrt{[1 - (A/A_1)^2]}} \, C_d A \sqrt{2gH}$$

where K = the *approach factor*

A_1 = cross-sectional area of the fluid in the pipeline

and H = pressure-head difference across the orifice

Fig. 7.8

146

Example An orifice plate of diameter 50mm is located in a pipeline 75mm in diameter, to measure the flow rate of water. The pressure-head difference across the orifice is equivalent to 22m of water, and the coefficient of discharge is 0.64. Calculate the volume of water flowing per hour.

$$Q = \frac{1}{\sqrt{[1 - (A/A_1)^2]}} \; C_d A \sqrt{2gH}$$

where $A = (\pi/4) \times (0.05\,\text{m})^2 = 1.964 \times 10^{-3}\,\text{m}^2$

$\qquad A_1 = (\pi/4) \times (0.075\,\text{m})^2 = 4.413 \times 10^{-3}\,\text{m}^2 \qquad C_d = 0.64$

$\qquad H = 22\text{m}$ and $g = 9.81\,\text{m/s}^2$

$\therefore \; Q = \dfrac{1}{\sqrt{[1 - (1.964/4.413)^2]}} \times 0.64 \times 1.964 \times 10^{-3}\,\text{m}^2 \; \sqrt{(2 \times 9.81\,\text{m/s}^2 \times }$

$\qquad\qquad\qquad\qquad\qquad\qquad\qquad\qquad\qquad\qquad\qquad\qquad\qquad 22\text{m})$

$\qquad = 29.162 \times 10^{-3}\,\text{m}^3/\text{s}$

$\qquad = 29.162 \times 10^{-3}/\text{s} \times 3600\,\text{s/h}$

$\qquad = 105\,\text{m}^3/\text{h}$

i.e. the flow rate of water along the pipeline is $105\,\text{m}^3/\text{h}$.

7.11 Momentum of a jet

Momentum is the product of mass m and velocity v,

i.e.   momentum = mass x velocity

or   momentum = mv

which should be remembered.

The unit for momentum is the kilogram metre per second (kg m/s).

Let a jet of liquid of density ρ *(rho)* and flowing with velocity v have a cross-sectional area A. The volumetric flow rate, i.e. the volume of liquid flowing per unit time, is then given by

     volumetric flow rate = area of jet x velocity

$$= Av$$

and the mass flow rate, i.e. the mass of liquid flowing per unit time, is given by

     mass flow rate = density x volumetric flow rate

$$= \rho Av$$

$\therefore$ momentum of the liquid per unit time = mass flow rate x velocity

$$= \rho Av.v$$

$$= \rho Av^2$$

which should be remembered.

147

Example A jet of water has a diameter of 0.04 m and velocity 30 m/s. If the density of the water is 1000 kg/m³, calculate the momentum per second in the jet.

Momentum per unit time = $\rho A v^2$

where ρ = 1000 kg/m³ $A = (\pi/4) \times (0.04\,\text{m})^2 = 0.0013\,\text{m}^2$

and v = 30 m/s

∴   momentum per unit time = 1000 kg/m³ × 0.0013 m² × (30 m/s)²

= 1170 kgm/s per second

i.e. the momentum per second in the jet is 1170 kgm/s.

7.12 Impulse

An impulse is the product of force F and time t and is equal to the change in momentum (see section 5.4, *Engineering science for technicians vol. 2*, by I. McDonagh, G. Waterworth, and R.P. Phillips),

i.e.   impulse = change in momentum

or $Ft = m(v - u)$

where v and u are the final and initial velocities respectively,

∴ $F = \dfrac{m(v - u)}{t}$

i.e.   force = change in momentum per unit time in the same direction as the change

7.13 Force of a jet on a flat plate

If a jet of liquid impinges on a flat plate as shown in fig. 7.9, the liquid will disperse in radial directions, reducing the velocity of the jet in the original direction to zero; i.e., upon impact with the flat plate, the momentum of the liquid in the original direction is zero.

Fig. 7.9 Force of a jet on a flat plate

148

$$\text{Change in momentum per unit time} = \text{final momentum} - \text{initial momentum}$$

$$= 0 - \rho A v^2$$

$$= -\rho A v^2$$

The minus sign indicates that the direction of the change is in the opposite direction to the incoming jet.

But, $\dfrac{\text{change in momentum}}{\text{per unit time}} = \dfrac{\text{force in the direction of}}{\text{the change}}$

From Newton's third law of motion, i.e. to every force there is an equal and opposite force reacting, the *reaction* to the change in momentum per unit time will be the force on the plate,

i.e.   force on the plate = $\rho A v^2$

and is in the *same* direction as the incoming jet, *which should be remembered.*

Example   Oil of density 800 kg/m³ impinges on a flat plate with a velocity of 6 m/s. If the diameter of the jet is 20 mm, determine the force on the plate.

Force on the plate = $\rho A v^2$

where ρ = 800 kg/m³ $A = (\pi/4) \times (0.02 \text{ m})^2 = 0.000\,314 \text{ m}^2$

and v = 6 m/s

$\therefore$ force on the plate = $800 \text{ kg/m}^3 \times 0.000\,314 \text{ m}^2 \times (6 \text{ m/s})^2$

$$= 9 \text{ N}$$

i.e. the force on the plate is 9 N.

Exercises on chapter 7

In the following exercises, the density of water is 1000 kg/m³.

1   At a point in a horizontal pipeline, the water pressure is 2.2 bar and the velocity is 5 m/s. What is the specific energy in the water?   [232.5 J/kg]

2   Write down, in symbolic form, Bernoulli's equation in terms of 'head' of liquid, stating the name of and the units for each symbol.

   Oil is stored at a height of 6 m above the outlet nozzle. If the velocity of flow at the outlet is 9 m/s, determine the frictional resistance to flow in terms of head of oil.   [1.87 m]

3   The pressure and velocity of a liquid at a point in a pipeline were found to be 3 bar and 17.5 m/s respectively. At a second point in the line, 5 m above the first point, the pressure and velocity were 2.8 bar and 14 m/s respectively. If the relative density of the liquid is 1.2, find the loss of head.   [2.32 m]

4 Water with a velocity of 10 m/s enters a pipeline at a point 50 m above the outlet. If the diameter of the outlet pipe is 0.2 m and the loss of head due to friction is 5.5 m, calculate the inlet diameter of the pipe.   [0.353 m]

5 In a pumped-storage hydroelectric scheme, water is raised 300 m from the lower to the upper reservoir. If the frictional losses are equivalent to a head of 35 m, find the pressure in the pump required to maintain a volumetric flow rate of 270 000 litres per minute through a 0.8 m diameter exit port at the pump. (1 litre = 10^{-3} m^3.)   [3.25 MN/m^2]

6 The surface of the water in a supply chamber is maintained at a constant height of 3.5 m above the outlet orifice, which is 10 mm in diameter. If there are no frictional losses, determine the volume of water issuing from the orifice in litres per minute.   [39.1 litres/min]

7 It is required to spray water on to a fire from a height of 12 m above the fire-hose nozzle. Determine the velocity of the water issuing from the nozzle. If frictional losses cause a pressure drop of 0.2 bar between the pump and the nozzle outlet, what is the pump pressure?   [15.34 m/s; 1.38 bar]

8 Water leaves a pump at a pressure of 2.5 bar and issues through a nozzle 15 mm in diameter at a distance of 150 m from the pump. If the pressure drop in the pipeline is 0.02 kN/m^2 per metre, calculate (a) the velocity of the water at exit from the nozzle, (b) the force the water jet would exert on a flat surface perpendicular or normal to the jet.   [22.23 m/s; 87.3 N]

9 A jet of water of diameter 40 mm impinges on a flat plate with a force of 200 N. If the plate is normal to the jet, what is the velocity of the water? [12.6 m/s]

10 A water jet flowing at the rate of 200 litres per minute strikes a flat plate, exerting on it a force of 50 N. What is the velocity of the water? [15 m/s]

11 A jet of water impinges normally on a fixed flat plate with a force of 600 N. If the velocity of the water on impact is 15 m/s, calculate the flow of water in litres per minute.   [2400 litres/min]

12 Water, issuing from a nozzle 20 mm in diameter, impinges normally on a fixed flat plate. If the water is supplied from a container which is maintained at a constant height of 20 m above the nozzle, calculate the force on the plate. Neglect frictional losses.   [123.3 N]

13 Water enters a pipeline with a pressure of 300 kPa and negligible velocity and leaves through a nozzle 100 mm in diameter, 20 m below the entry point. If the frictional losses are equivalent to a head of 6.5 m, determine the force the water will exert on a flat plate which is normal to the nozzle exit.   [6793 N]

14 A pipeline, full of water, tapers from 0.7 m diameter at point A to 0.35 m diameter at point B which is 25 m vertically below A. If at point A the pressure and velocity are 600 kPa and 5 m/s respectively, calculate the velocity at B. If the frictional head loss is 3.6 m, what will be the pressure at B?   [20 m/s; 622.4 kPa]

15 Water flows through a horizontal pipeline at the rate of 785.4 kg/s. If the mean velocity of the flow is 4 m/s, what is the diameter of the pipe? If the pipeline is 3 km long, determine the pump pressure required to maintain the flow rate if the frictional losses amount to 0.002 m per metre run of pipeline.   [0.5 m; 58.86 kN/m²]

16 In an experiment to determine the coefficients of discharge, velocity, and contraction for a sharp-edged orifice, the following data were obtained:

diameter of orifice   7.5 mm
head of water above centre of orifice   1.3 m
mass of water collected in 5 minutes   42.5 kg
horizontal displacement of jet in vertical height of 310 mm   1.2 m

Find the values of the coefficients and hence estimate the diameter of the jet at the vena contracta.   [C_d = 0.63; C_v = 0.95; C_c = 0.66; 6.09 mm]

17 The coefficients of velocity and contraction for a sharp-edged orifice having a diameter of 25 mm are 0.96 and 0.65 respectively. Water issues through the orifice on to the surface of a pool which is 2 m below the centre of the orifice. If the water strikes the surface at a horizontal distance of 6.2 m from the vena contracta, find (a) the head of water above the centre of the orifice, (b) the volumetric flow rate in m³/min.   [5.21 m; 0.185 m³/min]

18 An orifice plate having an orifice diameter of 60 mm is inserted in a pipe-line to measure the flow rate of water. If the approach factor is 1.25, calculate the diameter of the pipeline. Given that the coefficient of discharge is 0.65 and the pressure difference across the orifice is equivalent to 15 m of water, find the volumetric flow rate in m³/min.   [77.46 mm; 2.36 m³/min]

19 An orifice plate inserted in a pipeline carrying water is calibrated by com-paring the actual flow rate with the pressure-head difference across the plate. During the test, the following results were obtained:

diameter of pipeline   100 mm
diameter of orifice   60 mm
volume of water collected   3588 litres
duration of test   5 minutes
pressure difference across plate   2 m of water

From the results, calculate the approach factor and the coefficient of discharge. Estimate the flow rate in litres/minute when the pressure difference across the orifice is 1.2 m of water.   [1.072; 0.63; 556 litres/min]

Index